THE ROYAL FAMILY VS 'THE CROWN'

For my wonderful little Pippa, with all the love in the world.

THE ROYAL FAMILY VS 'THE CROWN'

Separating Fact from Fiction

CATHERINE CURZON

PEN & SWORD HISTORY

AN IMPRINT OF PEN & SWORD BOOKS LTD.
YORKSHIRE - PHILADELPHIA

First published in Great Britain in 2025 by
PEN AND SWORD HISTORY
An imprint of
Pen & Sword Books Ltd
Yorkshire – Philadelphia

ISBN 978 1 39905 957 2

A CIP catalogue record for this book is available from the British Library.

Typeset in Times New Roman 11.5/14 by
SJmagic DESIGN SERVICES, India.
Printed and bound in the United States of America by
Integrated Books International.

The Publisher's authorised representative in the EU for product safety is
Authorised Rep Compliance Ltd., Ground Floor, 71 Lower Baggot Street, Dublin
D02 P593, Ireland.
www.arccompliance.com

For a complete list of Pen & Sword titles please contact:
PEN & SWORD BOOKS LIMITED
George House, Units 12 & 13, Beevor Street, Off Pontefract Road,
Barnsley, South Yorkshire, S71 1HN, England
E-mail: enquiries@pen-and-sword.co.uk
Website: www.pen-and-sword.co.uk
or
PEN AND SWORD BOOKS
1950 Lawrence Rd, Havertown, PA 19083, USA
E-mail: uspen-and-sword@casematepublishers.com
Website: www.penandswordbooks.com

Contents

Contents

Image Credits

Images 1, 2, 5, 10, 12, 13, 17: Fotocollectie Anefo, public domain.

Images 3, 14: Wellcome Collection, public domain.

Image 4: Library of Congress Prints and Photographs Division, public domain.

Images 6, 8, 11: Public domain.

Image 7: Daily Herald Archive at the National Media Museum, public domain.

Image 9: Library of Congress, public domain.

Image 15: Mr BJ Daventry, Royal Air Force Official Photographer, public domain.

Image 16: NASA, public domain.

Image 18: Allan Warren, CC BY SA 3.0.

Image 19: Ben Salter/Oxyman/Wikimedia Commons, CC BY 2.0.

Image 20: John Hill, CC BY-SA 4.0.

Image 21: Margaret Thatcher Foundation, copyrighted free use.

Image 22: John MacIntyre/Paisley Scotland, CC BY 2.0.

Image 23: HM Government, OGL 3.

Image 24: The United States Army Band, CC BY 2.0.

Image 25: Bobak Ha'Eri/Wikimedia Commons, CC BY 2.5.

Image 26: Eva Rinaldi/Wikimedia Commons, CC BY SA 2.0.

Image 27: Abi Skipp/Wikimedia Commons, CC BY 2.0.

Image 28: Luigi Novi/Nightscream/Wikimedia Commons, CC BY 3.0.

Image 29: Northern Ireland Office, CC BY 2.0.

Image 30: Isaac Mayne/DCMS, PDM-Owner.

Image 31: Magnus D/Wikimedia Commons, CC BY 2.0.

Behind *The Crown*

Peter Morgan's smash-hit Netflix series, *The Crown*, is the latest offering in the distinguished royal line which bears his name. Morgan's first brush with the House of Windsor came in his acclaimed 2006 feature film *The Queen*, before expanding into 2013's *The Audience*, a hit stage play dramatising Queen Elizabeth II's meetings with the many prime ministers who held office during her record-breaking reign. *The Crown* is the spiritual successor to those enormously successful projects, expanding the scope to tell the story of her whole reign: a right royal undertaking. Over six seasons – so far – *The Crown* has followed the epoch-defining monarch through tumultuous times, from her days as a young princess through public triumph and private tragedy all the way into the twenty-first century and the next generation of monarchy.

When Netflix announced *The Crown*, speculation was immediately rife regarding who would clinch the plum roles. With each change of era and attendant change of cast, that speculation returned as feverishly as ever. Whether starring Claire Foy, Olivia Colman or Imelda Staunton, millions of devoted viewers have followed the ups and downs of the royal family, bewitched by the dramatised glimpse behind closed doors.

And dramatised is the keyword, because one thing *The Crown* has never claimed to be is documentary. Because so much of the series takes place behind those closed palace doors, there's always going to be a degree of dramatic license, but just how much of *The Crown* is dramatic license and how much is outright fiction? Season by season, episode by episode, this book will uncover what's fact, what's fiction and what lies somewhere in between.

Of course, this won't be an exhaustive investigation into every word spoken, every ornament and every medal, nor who sat where at various weddings, funerals and coronations, because that would run to volumes. Instead, it's a quick reference guide for fans to dip into when they fancy the inside scoop on the facts behind their favourite dramatic moments. So, did the foreign secretary really shoot up on his way to vital talks, did the Duke of Edinburgh balk at kneeling for his wife's coronation and did Princess Margaret face an impossible choice between love and duty? What really happened between Diana and a dashing heart surgeon and why did Queen Elizbeth II drag her heels when it came to visiting the victims of the Aberfan tragedy? And just *what* was the bit about the tampon? Fire up Netflix, get comfy on your throne and polish the crown jewels later, because when it comes to fact versus fiction, *The Royal Family vs 'The Crown'* has got you covered.

Seasons 1 and 2

Notable Cast

Princess Elizabeth/Queen Elizabeth II	Claire Foy
Prince Philip, Duke of Edinburgh	Matt Smith
Queen Mary	Eileen Atkins
Graham Sutherland	Stephen Dillane
Antony-Armstrong Jones	Matthew Goode
Queen Elizabeth The Queen Mother	Victoria Hamilton
King George VI	Jared Harris
Prince Edward, Duke of Windsor	Alex Jennings
Princess Margaret	Vanessa Kirby
Harold Macmillan	Anton Lesser
Winston Churchill	John Lithgow
Peter Townsend	Ben Miles
Anthony Eden	Jeremy Northam
Tommy Lascelles	Pip Torrens
Clementine Churchill	Harriet Walter
Wallis, Duchess of Windsor	Lia Williams
Louis, 1st Earl Mountbatten of Burma	Greg Wise

SEASON 1

1.1 Wolferton Splash

The Crown

As King George VI experiences the first symptoms of the illness that will kill him, Princess Elizabeth enchants the nation at her fairy-tale wedding to Philip, whilst ambitious politicians jockey for position. The groom's career in the Royal Navy takes the newlyweds to Malta, where they become parents and enjoy a carefree family life.

Back home, Winston Churchill returns to Downing Street, Princess Margaret flirts with her father's loyal retainer and Elizabeth and Philip's marriage comes under strain when the king's illness compels them to return to England and give up the military life for duty. Though few people know it, King George VI is dying.

The Truth

The first episode of the first season of *The Crown* has got a whole lot to pack in and, as we'll increasingly find as the seasons pass, it concerns itself largely with male stories. In fact, though we might expect Her Majesty Queen Elizabeth II to be the central character, that isn't always the case. Season after season, at least as much screen time is given to Philip's efforts to carve out his own role as is given to the queen's own triumphs and tribulations. It's perhaps not surprising, then, that much of the first episode tells the story of men. Indeed, the much-anticipated premiere episode opens not with Princess Elizabeth but with Philippos Andreou of Schleswig-Holstein-Sonderberg-Glücksburg, Prince of Greece and Denmark, better known to history as Prince Philip, Duke of Edinburgh.

As his ambitious and social climbing uncle, Louis Mountbatten, Earl Mountbatten of Burma, looks on with undisguised triumph, Philip renounces his Greek and Danish titles and privileges and is invested as Duke of Edinburgh in preparation for his marriage to Princess Elizabeth. In the wake of World War Two, Teutonic familial connections were still fraught with controversy and the prince did indeed assume his British mother's surname of Mountbatten, which it was hoped would make him more palatable to the subjects his wife would one day rule. Likewise, Philip did renounce his titles and privileges, little suspecting just how soon he would be called upon to surrender his career in the Royal Navy for life as a royal consort instead. Although *Wolferton Splash* shows Philip being naturalised as a Brit as he receives the Order of the Garter, that process was already completed in March, prior to this scene taking place.

Whilst the sight of King George VI (known as Bertie to his family and friends) reciting filthy limericks with his equerry, Group Captain Peter Townsend, is an aspect that one might naturally assume to be a product of the writer's imagination, it's anything but. Though it might be difficult to imagine the famously timid family man reciting obscene poems to take his mind off his concerns, the monarch absolutely loved a mucky limerick. It's worth noting, however, that this particular example was dreamed up by the scriptwriter rather than the king and the group captain. Less accurate are ominous hints about the sovereign's declining health as early as 1947; in fact, he didn't scale back his duties until 1948. When he did, it was due to a complaint in his leg, rather than his lungs.

Just as the show depicts, Philip was regarded in some quarters as a match unworthy of the heir to the throne, but Elizabeth and he married for love, not duty. The couple's friendship began in 1939, when the 13-year-old princess toured the grounds of Britannia Royal Naval College in Dartmouth. During this visit she was introduced to Philip, at the time a dashing cadet five years her senior; he made a heck of an impact. The couple wrote to one another throughout the war and Elizabeth, it seems, never seriously considered anyone else as a potential match. When the time came to think about husbands she did indeed lobby for the man she wanted and, just as *The Crown*'s Churchill grumbles, when the princess included *obey* in the wedding vows, it was at her own insistence. The word had been omitted from the vows for nearly two decades by that point, yet Princess Elizabeth uttered it when she tied the knot in Westminster Abbey on 20 November 1947.

Whilst Churchill's ranting about Nazis in the Abbey might be a little bit of showmanship, it serves to inform the viewer of the reality of the prince's family long before it comes under the spotlight in season two. It's important to be clear that Philip never had any Nazi sympathies himself, but his turbulent early years did see him wash up in Nazi Germany briefly in his teens, where his sisters married men who had ties to the party. In fact, Philip's sister Sophie even named her child Karl Adolf, in honour of Hitler.

In a few seasons we'll see Philip's mother, Princess Alice of Greece and Denmark, headline her very own episode, but her appearance in the premiere is fleeting if memorable. Dismissed by a catty Queen Mary and Queen Elizabeth, later to become the Queen Mother, as "the hun nun", Princess Alice cuts an eccentric figure amid the splendour in her grey nun's garb, but this is where fact and fiction part company. Though she attended Elizabeth's coronation wearing a silky and somewhat more designer version of her nun's habit, Princess Alice did not found her holy order until 1949, two years after the wedding. Official marriage portraits show her dressed in a formal gown and displaying her royal orders, not clad in a religious habit.

And then there's the name calling. The Queen Mother would've been very aware that Princess Alice was born at Windsor Castle in the presence of Queen Victoria, so she would certainly never have referred to her as a "hun". In fact, the person to whom she did playfully apply the nickname was actually Philip himself. By all accounts, he found it hilarious.

Wolferton Splash has got a lot of ground to cover, so it's no surprise that we get a little bit of shorthand: expect a lot more of this as the years fly by. We see Anthony Eden's narrow-eyed resentment of Churchill, who refuses to relinquish the throne of the Conservative Party to the younger, more polished Eden, and there are hints at the Road Runner, Wile E Coyote dynamic between them that will develop over the next few episodes. Eden and Churchill's careers and lives were entwined for decades; indeed, Eden's second wife – glimpsed in *The Crown* as a silent figure in expensive millinery – was a member of the Churchill family, and the two men were close colleagues and bitter rivals. It's true, however, that when Winston Churchill was returned to office in 1951, his wife, Clementine, did have her doubts about the wisdom of the move. Her husband was in his seventies and his health was flagging.

She knew all too well the price that the stress of leading the country might exact on the man she loved.

Winston Churchill and Anthony Eden first met just after the First World War, when Eden was a student at Oxford and Churchill a minister in Lloyd George's Liberal cabinet. Just a couple of decades later Eden was a high-flier in Churchill's cabinet, carrying with him his mentor's promise that he would see out the war then hand over the reins of power. Yet once peacetime came and Churchill clung onto his position as leader of the Conservative Party even after the electorate voted him out of Downing Street, Eden began to wonder if his day would ever come. When it finally did, his brief time at number 10 was to prove catastrophic.

But all of this is yet to come. For now, the on-screen Princess Elizabeth and Philip (it would be another decade before he was invested as a British prince) are enjoying life as young newlyweds. Though the queen did later indulge a love of making home movies, the cinecamera that Elizabeth receives as a wedding present from her father is sadly inaccurate. She actually received a sapphire and diamond necklace and earring set.

Five years pass in the blink of an eye thanks to a time-lapsing home-movie montage and the happy couple are soon enjoying a carefree life in Malta. By the time the montage ends, we've seen two new arrivals join the family – Charles and Anne. However, though the children are shown in Malta, they actually stayed at home in the UK rather than join their parents overseas. And it's at home that trouble is brewing.

Just as *Wolferton Splash* shows, when the king fell ill his doctors determined that the monarch's left lung must be removed, a procedure that they hoped would allay the progress of what later proved to be terminal cancer. When the operation was recorded in his notes, the king's privacy was maintained by his doctors mentioning only "structural changes" in his lung. It's correct that the 1951 procedure to remove the monarch's lung took place in Buckingham Palace and it's equally true that afterwards the king started to wear rouge in order to affect a healthy pallor. Following the debilitating operation, it's likely that King George knew that he was entering the final stages of his life; however, though the series shows Bertie receiving a terminal diagnosis, history doesn't record how much his doctors actually told him about the likely outcome.

Mindful that his daughter and her husband will soon be Queen and consort, the king asks the couple to undertake an official Commonwealth tour on his behalf. Confronted with Philip's resentment that he has been pulled off active duty and left with nothing better to do than renovate Clarence House, Bertie gives him a fatherly talking to about the life of service that awaits him. Duty, as we shall learn, is a key theme that runs through *The Crown*, along with a generous dollop of resentment. Elizabeth's breezy assertion that her children won't miss them when they're away for months on end will, we know, come back to haunt her both in her relationship with Charles and his connection with his own sons. If *The Crown* does one thing very well indeed, it's foreshadowing. Though *The Crown* incorrectly shows Charles and Anne living in Malta, the children were already well used to life without their parents.

During the final Christmas the royal family spent together at Sandringham before the king's death, Group Captain Peter Townsend chose to join them rather than celebrate with his own family. *Wolferton Splash* uses this as an excuse to show Princess Margaret making eyes at the dashing Battle of Britain hero, hinting at the drama their relationship will ignite. Even as Elizabeth warns her sister off, we know that their romance will shake the nation. Yet Townsend was a loyal retainer and had enormous respect and affection for George VI. Knowing of his employer's ill health, his presence that Christmas was as much a matter of duty as it was motivated by his desire to see Margaret, though that was certainly part of it. The episode ends with Princess Elizabeth sitting at the king's desk behind his ominous official red box, little suspecting how soon his cares and those of the Commonwealth will become hers.

1.2 Hyde Park Corner

The Crown

Whilst Princess Elizabeth and the Duke of Edinburgh enjoy a royal tour of Africa, at home the king's condition is worsening. Churchill battles Anthony Eden's efforts to unseat him in Downing Street and learns that his foreign secretary has even made an audacious approach to George VI.

The king's death plunges the royal household into mourning. As courtiers jostle for position, Princess Margaret turns to Townsend for support and they begin their affair. Recalled from her tour, a heartbroken Elizabeth is now the Queen. It is the start of a brand new era.

The Truth

Let's start with an easy win. Hyde Park Corner was indeed the coded phrase to be used when King George VI died, so it's a fitting title for this particular episode.

It's all change for Princess Elizabeth and the Duke of Edinburgh, who start their first official tour amid murmurings of colonial independence. The episode loses no time in showing us that Philip is still far from ready to assume the gravitas of a monarch's consort as he makes tone deaf jokes at the expense of their hosts, including asking a Kikuyu chieftain if he had stolen his Victoria Cross. It's a nod to one of the Duke of Edinburgh's most headline-grabbing habits: off colour remarks. Whilst Philip was no stranger to speaking his mind, it's unlikely that a man with such an affinity for matters military would have made such a thundering faux pas. As *The Crown* later shows, the Duke of Edinburgh was a stickler for showing proper respect when it came to such things.

The lines between fact and fiction aren't so much blurred as eradicated in London, where Foreign Secretary Anthony Eden and Lord Salisbury, aka Bobbety, are scheming to bring about the removal of Churchill. *The Crown* has the unctuous Eden approach the king at Sandringham to ask him to exercise his constitutional right and remove the prime minister from office on account of incapacity, the evidence for which seems to be Churchill bringing his dogs into cabinet meetings and bellowing dictation at his secretaries from his bathtub. Whilst Eden certainly waited in the wings for Churchill to leave the stage, he never sought the monarch's assistance to wield the hook and he was far too adept a politician to attempt such blatant and blundering manipulation.

Of course, the awkward exchange between the duplicitous Eden and the gently admonishing King George serves as a reminder that, though Eden could afford to be patient and seize his moment when the time was right, the king had no such luck. He had never wanted to wear the crown, but was forced to do so when his brother abdicated: some seek power, some have it thrust upon them. The on-screen Eden has no such reservations about assuming power, but it's unlikely that he allowed himself to be meaningfully persuaded into Winston Churchill's chair at the cabinet table as he does in *Hyde Park Corner*. Eden was a consummate and experienced politician who, alongside Churchill, had steered the nation through the Second World War. As an enormously talented foreign secretary and highly experienced deputy prime minister, he knew better than to show his hunger so clearly.

Whilst we're discussing political fictions in *The Crown*, Churchill conducting his business from the bathtub isn't something the scriptwriters dreamed up, but one of his most adoring staff members is. Venetia Scott, the unfortunate secretary who has to sit on the floor outside the Downing Street bathroom as Churchill bellows out his points of order, is an entirely fictional character who has been drafted in for a very specific purpose indeed. She will, of course, play a significant role a little later in the first season.

Though we shall investigate the Margaret/Townsend affair in more detail further down the line, whilst there's no denying that the heartbroken princess's dramatic horseback flight from her father's death is cinematic in the extreme, it's also likely fictional. She and Townsend grew closer than ever as Margaret mourned her father and it's fair to say that the heartbroken flight, followed by that passionate and forbidden kiss, really do get the message across that this is an affair that can only cause trouble. Margaret was 14 when she and Peter Townsend first met, but their romance didn't begin until soon after the death of the late king. Townsend was 16 years older than the princess and had enjoyed a distinguished military career. He was also a husband and father, though the Townsend marriage eventually ended after his wife had an affair of her own. One day, the romance between the princess and the dashing Group Captain would grip the nation.

Margaret also features in a scene that chilled audiences, as she stumbles into her late father's bedroom only to find him being embalmed. Though the king's remains were prepared for burial at Windsor, there's no record of the princess being present at any stage of the gruesome process. What the scene serves to demonstrate is just how alone and confused the youngest princess is, trapped in rain-drenched England whilst her sister suns herself in Kenya. As *the Crown* suggests, it's little wonder that she turned to the dependable Peter Townsend for comfort.

And speaking of Kenya, Elizabeth and Philip did indeed enjoy a romantic stopover at Treetops, but sadly there were no marauding elephants for the Duke of Edinburgh to chase away. However, the episode does offer a nice nod to the princess's experience as a mechanic during World War Two, when she waves aside a crowd of confused men who are clustered around an incapacitated jeep, and ably diagnoses the problem in a few seconds. Scenes in which the British authorities scramble to reach the new queen to tell her of her father's death before she hears it from someone else are mostly true, however, as Elizabeth really was out of contact during her travels in Kenya. Her black mourning dress, meanwhile, had already gone on ahead of her to the next stop on the tour, meaning that one had to be delivered to her on the runway as soon as her plane touched down in England. That oversight led to a change in royal protocol that persists to this day: whenever the royals travel, their mourning attire stays with them.

Whilst the speech Winston Churchill reads to the nation following the late king's death is as moving today as it ever was, it's a fiction that the cabinet gathered together to listen, just as it is a fiction that Eden stormed out of the room, having pinned his hopes on Churchill making a hash of this most important of occasions. If there's one thing Winston Churchill could be relied upon to do well, it was to deliver a speech.

Perhaps one of the most ill-served characters in *The Crown* is Tommy Lascelles, the unflappable Private Secretary to the monarch. Though in reality he was a trusted and pragmatic retainer to whom the royals often turned for help and advice, *The Crown* reimagines him as a lurking figure of sinister intent, who exists only to put the family in their place and keep them there with weaponised protocol. The scenes in which he tries to force Townsend to leave the royal household after catching him in a tryst with Princess Margaret are entirely false. In fact, in Lascelles's diaries he spoke with warmth, understanding and sympathy about the situation Townsend was in, whilst also observing that the equerry was rather too enmeshed in the drama for his own good. Though it's true that Elizabeth had to give up her secretary, Martin Charteris, in favour of Lascelles when she succeeded to the throne, Lascelles didn't scheme against Charteris. Instead, it was simply the established order of things: Charteris would not have expected to serve as secretary to Elizabeth now she was the queen, but knew instead that he simply had to wait for his turn to come. But *The Crown* needs its villains and for now, they are Eden and Lascelles.

There are broader themes in episode two that defy efforts to place them in the fact or fiction category. It's not too much of a stretch to imagine that Philip found his sudden promotion from husband to consort something of a lurch, but he was born royal and would have been prepared for the role that awaited him. However, it certainly was an upsetting of the accepted social order of the 1950s. Whether it needed to be quite such a dominant theme is something we'll return to.

The episode ends on one of the standout scenes of the series, as the elderly Queen Mary travels to Sandringham to curtsey to her granddaughter, now sovereign. The curtsey did happen, though it was at Clarence House. Both in *The Crown* as in reality, it serves as a powerful symbol that the old order had given way to the new.

1.3 Windsor

The Crown

After an opening flashback to King Edward VIII delivering his abdication speech, the former king, now Duke of Windsor, returns to England to attend his brother's funeral. There he finds an unwelcoming family, but the queen turns out to be an unlikely ally and she's in need of some advice.

With quibbles over the name of the new royal house and the place in which Elizabeth and Philip will make their family home rumbling away, Churchill decides to apply some pressure to the fledgling monarch. Little does he know that the Queen has a few cards of her own to play.

The Truth

When it comes to fiction, Edward and Mrs Simpson seem to come as something of a package deal, and that's exactly how *The Crown* plays it too. In reality, Wallis was in Cannes awaiting her divorce when the departing Edward VIII (David to those closest to him) made his abdication speech, but *Windsor* makes much of her shadowy presence in the room at her man's side. Likewise, whilst *The Crown* shows him signing the Instrument of Abdication immediately before he makes his speech, the two events took place a day apart.

Edward was Prince of Wales when he met American Wallis Simpson, a married socialite who was part of his champagne-swilling set. Rumours regarding the nature of their relationship were swirling by 1934, though the prince was swift to deny that they were anything other than friends. However, soon after his succession to the throne in 1936, the new king confessed that he was in love with Mrs Simpson. With one divorce under her belt and another looming, Wallis was not considered a suitable bride for the head of the Church of England, which didn't acknowledge a marriage if one party's former spouse was still living. When Edward became king, Wallis's first ex-husband was still alive and her second soon-to-be-ex-husband very definitely was. Faced with a choice between marriage and the throne, Edward chose the former. He abdicated in favour of his younger brother, King George VI. All of this will cast a very dark shadow over *The Crown*.

Despite being ostensibly about the queen, this is another episode that seems more concerned with Philip's lack of meaningful purpose, demonstrated here by his wish to remain in Clarence House rather than move to Buckingham Palace, and to call the royal house the House of Mountbatten, much to the delight of his ambitious uncle Louis. This is a cocktail of fact and fiction. Philip's life had been rather transitory since childhood and he had lived variously in Greece, France, Germany and the United Kingdom. With his father largely absent and his mother having been diagnosed with schizophrenia, he spent more time in school or with members of his extended family than he did with either parent. Mountbatten, Philip's maternal uncle, took his nephew under his wing just as he would later counsel Prince Charles, serving his own ambitions even as he was a mentor and guide for the two younger men.

As *The Crown* suggests, the young Philip hadn't really had anything like a permanent home before marriage saw him settled at Clarence House, and it's no secret that Buckingham Palace isn't exactly a cosy place. Leaky, cold and more like an office building and hospitality complex than a family home, it's little surprise that no royal has been particularly keen to live there. As Tommy Lascelles and Winston Churchill are united in believing, though, it is the monarch's seat and tradition must be observed.

When it comes to the matter of names, there's certainly some truth in the suggestion that Mountbatten toasted the future of the House of Mountbatten a little prematurely. However, when he did so he was simply following the established order, as a queen's royal house usually does assume the name of her husband. When word of his plans reached Queen Mary, she ensured that it was passed along to Winston Churchill. He balked at the prospect of disturbing the continuity of the House of Windsor, the royal family that had cemented its place in the hearts of the nation by seeing out the war in London rather than fleeing for the safety of a remote hideaway. One thing the series does depict accurately is Philip's annoyance when he heard the news, though he had favoured the House of Edinburgh over that of Mountbatten. Harold Macmillan recalled that the Duke of Edinburgh made a strong argument for the House of Edinburgh, but found himself overruled. The House of Windsor won out, though Queen Elizabeth II did not make the dramatised speech to the Privy Council that *Windsor* shows.

Much is made in this episode of the fact that Churchill wished to delay the coronation by sixteen months, seemingly because he knew that the ambitious Eden wouldn't dare to unseat him whilst he was planning the ceremony. This is untrue; the only reason George VI's coronation was held so soon after his succession was because he used the date already reserved for his brother. In reality, the coronation date for Queen Elizabeth II had always been planned for 1953: the amount of time required to arrange such a showstopping event is immense. This, of course, is the card that sends the dramatic house falling. If the coronation wasn't delayed to save Churchill, then the queen couldn't have leveraged that fact to make demands of her prime minister, as she does in the episode. We are very definitely on Planet *Crown*.

If this installment belongs mainly to the Duke of Edinburgh, then the Duke of Windsor is certainly the other focal point. Hardly known for his erudite manner and philosophical counselling, *The Crown* reimagines him as the Yoda of Buckingham Palace, dispensing wisdom and good advice to his niece as to why she should follow Churchill's recommendations. Though it's true that the prime minister was sympathetic to the duke's decision to give up everything for love, to depict the former monarch as a fount of sagacity is doing the hedonistic David a great favour indeed. A far from flattering portrait of the playboy prince can be found in the diaries of Tommy Lascelles, who despaired of Edward as selfish, childish and self-obsessed. Lascelles concluded that the Duke of Windsor was driven by a craven wish for money and pleasure above all things and that he was incapable of feeling true affection for anyone.

When it comes to the Duke and Duchess of Windsor's spiteful nicknames for the royal family, it's truth all the way. The Queen Mother really was 'Cookie' and Elizabeth 'Shirley Temple', whilst the Queen Mother referred to Wallis Simpson scathingly as 'that woman'. It's also true that the duke's rejection of the crown quite understandably led to bad feeling in the family. Indeed, the Queen Mother never forgave him for his abdication and firmly believed that the stress of being monarch destroyed the health of her sensitive husband, eventually hastening his early death. Later, the Duke of Windsor would suggest that the Queen Mother's dislike of him sprang from the fact that she was, in fact, in love with him rather than with her husband. He always did have a healthy ego. Incidentally, whilst Wallis's husbands were alive at the time of the abdication, Churchill is mistaken in his belief that they both lived to see Elizabeth succeed to the throne. Earl Winfield Spencer Jr, her first husband, died in 1950.

Though the duke might not have spent much time dispensing the sort of wisdom he bestows upon the young queen in *Windsor*, the scenes of him travelling first class and dressing in the sharpest suits whilst pleading poverty are certainly accurate. The Duke and Duchess of Windsor lived what might be termed a jet setting life, even though the duke was particularly keen to make the point that he was a man of deeply reduced circumstances despite his immense wealth. Equally true is the fact that Wallis Simpson never received the HRH she so coveted: it was simply a step too far for the royal family, who held firm even when the Duke of Windsor made an empty threat never to return to England unless the title was granted. To the end, the queen refused to agree to his demands, so what became his dying wish remained forever unfulfilled.

In *Windsor* and many times throughout the first season, Elizabeth rues the fact that she was forced to become queen thanks to her uncle's abdication. Yet the abdication of the childless Edward VIII didn't change the line of succession at all: George VI was always his brother's heir and Elizabeth was heir to her father. In reality, the Duke of Windsor didn't die until 1972. Therefore, if Edward VIII hadn't abdicated the throne, this is the earliest Elizabeth would have succeeded, provided that her father didn't live longer in this changed timeline. Had Edward VIII remained on the throne, married someone other than Wallis and fathered legitimate heirs of his own, of course, the royal family would look very different indeed.

Meanwhile, Tommy Lascelles schemes and Peter Townsend continues to be all things to all people, serving chiefly as Margaret's lover and Philip's flying instructor. Philip did learn to fly, though it wasn't with Townsend. However, these scenes serve to show just how close the equerry was growing to the family, even if Philip addresses Townsend with matey familiarity, whilst the WW2 ace is forced to follow formal protocol. Life as Princess Margaret's paramour won't be easy.

1.4 Act of God

The Crown

As the great smog envelops London, the population struggle to go about their daily life in the midst of the environmental catastrophe. Despite the cost to the city, Churchill refuses to intervene or even discuss the crisis with Cabinet, instead blaming an act of God for the disaster.

The queen's advisors press her to force Churchill to step down but when his advisor, Venetia Scott, is hit by a bus in the smog after visiting her ailing flatmate in hospital, the PM faces the true cost of his inaction. His decision to finally take decisive steps to tackle the pollution comes just in the nick of time. The queen refrains from asking him to step down, much to the annoyance of the thwarted Clement Atlee.

The Truth

Dramatic, moving and packed with incident? Yes. Factually accurate? Nowhere near.

Before we get into the murky matter of the London smog, there's a pre-credits sequence filled with derring-do as Group Captain Townsend and the Duke of Edinburgh take to the skies. Whilst it's true that Philip became a Marshall of the Royal Air Force, his assertion to Townsend that he received the honorary rank upon his marriage in 1947 isn't accurate. The Duke of Edinburgh received the rank in 1953, the year after this episode is set. It flags up an earlier error as the duke erroneously wore his RAF wings at his on-screen wedding, despite not receiving them until many years later.

Back at the palace we get a handy scene in which Queen Mary outlines the differences between herself, Queen Elizabeth The Queen Mother, and Queen Elizabeth II, to a confused maid. Any similarly confused audience members can now also relax. There were indeed three queens at this stage in history: Queen Mary, mother-in-law of Queen Elizabeth, herself the Queen Mother to the reigning Queen Elizabeth II.

This is one of those episodes that sticklers for historical accuracy better avoid unless they want their blood to boil. Whilst there was a serious smog that lasted for four days in December 1952, the scenes of chaos and collapse that greet viewers are a huge exaggeration versus the reality. Whilst it's estimated that somewhere between 4,000 and 12,000 people died, most of them with pre-existing health conditions, the episode's depiction of panic in the streets, a rampant crimewave and a health service on its knees are really there just to create the requisite backstory to lead the idealistic Venetia into danger. Although she is a fictional character herself, the bus that kills her must also be a work of fiction, because all public transport other than the tube was suspended due to the pea souper.

As a side note, in 2023 one major online UK news site actually referenced the death of Venetia Scott and its impact on Churchill as a point of fact, which might say more about the state of journalism than it does about the believability of *The Crown*.

Whilst it's true that Churchill was under fire during the smog, it wasn't because of his failure to act. Instead, the motion of censure which he narrowly survived accused him of a more general lack of ability, with smog not meriting a mention. It won't come as a surprise to learn that there's no evidence that Clement Atlee and Lord Mountbatten were scheming to use the smog to unseat the PM either, or that the queen was about to kick Churchill out of Downing Street as punishment for his inaction.

Act of God hammers home Churchill's undermining and overbearing attitude towards the young monarch, positing that their relationship began as combative and matured into mutual fondness. Churchill held the queen in the highest esteem and she returned the sentiment, grateful for the guidance and wisdom he had shared during the earliest days of her reign. In fact, when she attended the late prime minister's funeral, the queen arrived before Churchill's own family. Though protocol dictates that the monarch must always be the last person to arrive, it was important to Elizabeth to show due respect to the man she had so admired and his loved ones.

In one last bit of fiction, the ground-breaking Clean Air Acts actually came along in 1956 and 1968 respectively, not after a rip-roaring speech from the impassioned prime minister, newly fired up by grief and guilt. Ending on a positive note, though, the smog really was as thick and acrid as *The Crown* depicts; it was a turning point for the gravity with which air pollution was perceived in the British Isles.

1.5 Smoke and Mirrors

The Crown

We're flashing back again, this time to see young Princess Elizabeth as she helps her beloved father prepare for his own coronation in 1936. When we find ourselves back in the fifties, the Duke of Windsor is ready to raise hell since neither he nor his wife have been invited to the forthcoming coronation of the young queen.

Hoping to keep Philip busy, Elizabeth charges him with planning the celebrations, but few are anticipating the television spectacular the duke dreams up.

The Truth

As we hit the midpoint of the series, the stage is set for a real spectacle: the coronation of Queen Elizabeth II. However, once again this defining moment in the life of the young woman is told through the prism of her husband's dissatisfaction. Plus ça change. But let's kick off with another easy win: St Edward's Crown does indeed weigh five pounds, though the version worn by Elizabeth in this episode looks huge. It appears equally ginormous when her father tries it on in flashback, but perhaps this is to suggest the symbolic size of the burden.

Seventeen years after the abdication, the former Edward VIII, now Duke of Windsor, is keen to watch his niece receive her crown at Westminster Abbey. By now living in splendour in France, he returns to England to visit his ailing mother, Queen Mary. It's a relatively small point but in fact he travelled from New York and was accompanied during his visit by his sister, Mary, Princess Royal and Countess of Harewood. Incidentally, the Princess Royal was also one of the few members of the royal family who met Mrs Simpson, when the duke underwent optical surgery in London in 1965.

But onto *Smoke and Mirrors*.

Despite being in the UK out of familial duty, the Duke of Windsor is keen to secure an invite for himself and his wife to the Westminster Abbey coronation. His request takes everyone by surprise, whereas in reality the question of his attendance was one that had first been raised in 1952. After much to-and-froing, including conversations between the Archbishop of

Canterbury and the queen, it was agreed that the duke's presence at the coronation would be unacceptable. A letter was duly dispatched to inform the Duke of Windsor of the decision and, in all honesty, it's unlikely that he was surprised. In *The Crown*, of course, drama takes centre stage, as the furious duke puts on a sparkling display of oratory to lambast the Archbishop and politicians who have denied him his wish. One thing *The Crown* does capture is how much of a headache the abdicated king could be; Tommy Lascelles's diaries reveal plenty of clashes with the Duke of Windsor, who singularly failed to learn a single lesson in all his years.

The coronation of Queen Elizabeth II took place on 2 June 1953 and marked a watershed in not only the royal family's relationship with the media and public, but the history of television. More than 20 million viewers settled down to watch the live broadcast in pubs, homes and other locations, many having splashed out on their first television set specifically for the occasion. It was the first time that a television audience had outnumbered radio listeners in the United Kingdom.

The landmark BBC coverage placed cameras inside Westminster Abbey, allowing the public to watch a coronation for the very first time. Though Her Majesty's advisors had resisted the initiative, the queen herself championed the move and threw her support behind it, keen to show that she was a modern monarch. The coverage was shown across the globe and in the United States alone, 85 million viewers tuned in to witness history in the making.

Without a doubt the highlight of this episode is the montage that mingles real and dramatised coronation footage, setting the spectacle against scenes of the Duke and Duchess of Windsor's party in Paris, where they and their friends are among the millions watching the ceremony on television. This they did do; what it would have been to be a fly on the wall and hear the commentary at that party.

The Windsors had settled in the Château Le Bois in the 16th arrondissement of Paris in 1952 and it became their home for the rest of their lives. The house, later taken over by Mohamed Al-Fayed, was completely refitted to the personal specification of the duchess and was leased from the city of Paris for a peppercorn rent. I'm particularly delighted to confirm that the pug pillows glimpsed in season one are accurate, as was the couple's famous – some might say infamous - passion for jewels and fashion. The red leather dispatch box the duke proudly shows a visiting journalist reached its final chapter in 1998, when it was sold at auction by Sotheby's. It didn't, of course, bear the Prince of Wales feathers: the heir had succeeded to the throne, after all, even if he didn't hang onto it.

As the queen prepares to be crowned and the Duke of Windsor prepares to serve some sassy commentary to his guests, it is up to the Duke of Edinburgh to turn the spectacle into something more fitting of the modern era. He was actually appointed as chair of the Coronation Committee a year earlier than *The Crown* asserts, but fudging the timeline is par for the course by now. As chair, Philip was indeed a trailblazer who encouraged the televising of the coronation, much to the chagrin of the ecclesiastical lobby. *Smoke & Mirrors* makes a great deal of scenes in which he asks his wife to forego the requirement for him to kneel before her during the sacred ceremony. It is another cause of tension between them and another occurrence that we can safely assume didn't happen.

Once again, it's important to remember that the Duke of Edinburgh was born and raised in a royal household, so whilst it's super dramatic and a great source of conflict to suggest that he baulked at kneeling before his wife, it's also very likely to be made up. The duke knew precisely what he was getting into with his marriage and he wasn't someone who was raised as a regular Joe. He lived royal protocol from the day he was born: deference had been hardwired into him despite his famously irascible nature.

One last note of interest to viewers is the seamless intercutting between real footage of the coronation and recreated scenes. It's an impressive technical feat that really ties the fact and fiction together, though the coronation ceremony has been considerably filleted in order to give us and the rueful Duke of Windsor a sort of greatest hits, pageantry edition, to keep the episode bowling along. And of course, we do get our *Zadok the Priest*... it's just in the wrong place.

1.6 Gelignite

The Crown

As Philip parties with his freewheeling friends, for Peter Townsend and Princess Margaret, love is well and truly in the air. The queen is enthusiastically in favour of the couples' plans to wed, but Lascelles and the Queen Mother find themselves united in disapproval.

Elizabeth is shocked to discover that an eighteenth-century act means there can be no marriage without her permission unless Margaret waits for her 25th birthday, so she decides to play the long game. As the public unite behind the star-crossed lovers, Lascelles moves to have the fly in the ointment shipped out once and for all.

The Truth

Before we dive into heartbreak, you might be wondering if the Duke of Edinburgh and his chums really did carouse at riotous and boozy lunches. The answer is a resounding yes. The bawdy knees up enjoyed by the duke and Mike Parker is in fact a meeting of the Thursday Club, a society of men who got together to eat, drink and be merry. Once a week the club met in an upstairs room at Wheeler's in Soho's Old Compton Street under the stewardship of photographer Baron Nahum. Officially, it was all good clean fun; according to unofficial accounts, however, it was more like a weekly stag do.

Since Margaret and Townsend are the stars of this show, it's probably time for a quick summing up of the facts of their romance. It's also worth mentioning at this point that the queen's dazed expression when reminded of the Royal Marriages Act is certainly a bit of fiction. As a monarch with a younger sister and children of her own, she would've been well-versed in this particular bit of legislation, which came along in the eighteenth century in the wake of some seriously unsuitable royal marriages. The act requires the monarch to okay any union between a member of the royal family and their would-be spouse. If that consent isn't given then the royal concerned has to wait until they reach the age of 25, then apply to Parliament and the Privy Council for permission instead. Of course, that same dazed expression is supposed to hint at Elizabeth's lack of formal education, but her constitutional education as the heir to the throne was comprehensive.

Margaret and Townsend did fall in love and request permission to marry. *The Crown* posits that the queen initially okayed the match but, stung by the public's adoring reaction to Townsend, the spotlight that fell on her household and the pressure applied to her by the scheming and heartless Lascelles, she recanted and instead asked Margaret to wait until she turned 25. In *The Crown*, Her Majesty is aware that Townsend is set for a new posting in Brussels. She instructs Lascelles to bring the Group Captain's change of role forward and send him away whilst Margaret is occupied by a royal tour in Rhodesia. If *Gelignite* is to be believed, the sinister palace movers and shakers struck Townsend from his scheduled role on the visit to Rhodesia with Margaret in order to wrong foot the couple and keep them apart.

In reality, Townsend was due to go to Brussels before Margaret returned to England and the princess already knew of the plan. In addition, it was Churchill who encouraged the new posting even though he believed the romance should be allowed to proceed. *The Crown* has newspaper reports of the relationship between Margaret and Townsend take Churchill by surprise, whereas he actually knew about their affair before the press made it public. Whilst divorcee Anthony Eden, himself no stranger to heartbreak, was sympathetic to the affair, Churchill was pragmatic about its chances and said honestly that he doubted the cabinet would approve a marriage between the couple. Supposedly, Margaret later told Churchill's Private Secretary, Jock Colville, that between them Tommy Lascelles and Winston Churchill had ruined her life by preventing the marriage. In his diaries, Tommy accepts the accusation with his usual pragmatism, doubtful both of the statement and its veracity.

As is often the case in *The Crown*, the timeline is at best wayward, Townsend was divorced in November 1952 and informed Lascelles of his relationship with Princess Margaret the following month. When he did so, he told Lascelles that the Queen and the Duke of Edinburgh were already aware of the affair. In *Gelignite*, however, the revelation is moved forward into the second half of 1953.

One thing the episode gets right is the simple clue that gave away the couple: Princess Margaret really did brush a piece of lint off her lover's lapel, a curiously intimate act that caught everybody's eye. It was *The People* that broke the news after the American press had started to take notice, rather than *The Crown*'s *News Chronicle*. It's nice to see some real attention to detail in a series that can be pretty cavalier when it comes to dates: as shown on screen, the story broke on 14 June 1953. However, the paparazzi's rabid pursuit of Townsend during his visit to Northern Ireland with the queen is dramatic licence, as are scenes of the equerry playing up to and encouraging the photographers. Though there was undeniably press interest, Townsend didn't strike a pose for the cameras, nor did he provoke the royal wrath with any crowd pleasing antics.

When it comes to the details in *Gelignite*, truth and fiction are difficult to separate. Indeed, it rather depends on who you ask, because all the major players have a very different take on the situation. What's interesting is that one thing every version of events seems to agree on is that it was Churchill who advised Queen Elizabeth II not to consent to the marriage. Instead, he encouraged her to ask Margaret to wait two years so that royal permission would no longer be required. Curiously for a series that inserts Churchill at every opportunity, he is absent from the scheming and manoeuvring that tears the star-crossed lovers apart. The finger of blame is instead pointed at the queen, thus giving the scriptwriters a great excuse to drive a wedge between the sisters in the episodes to come.

So what of the princess and the equerry?

Despite the love the couple doubtless had for one another, there were strong factors working against them, not least Townsend's position as a commoner and a member of the royal household. He was much older than Princess Margaret and a divorcee at a time when the Church of England didn't recognise the marriages of those who were divorced as legitimate unions, rendering the couple's position even more precarious. With barely two decades separating the affair from that of Edward and Mrs Simpson, there was little chance that the marriage would receive sanction.

Whilst the queen did ask her sister to wait, she didn't do so out of spite, nor had she already intimated that she would give the match the official go ahead as the Royal Marriages Act required. Rather, she wanted Margaret to be sure that she was making the right decision and wasn't just swept up in the romance. The public really did fall for the love story of Margaret and Townsend, though. When the romance ended, it was inevitable that people would look for somewhere to place the blame.

1.7 Scientia Potentia Est

The Crown

Dismayed by news that the Soviet Union are conducting nuclear weapons tests, Churchill seeks a summit with John Foster Dulles, only to suffer a stroke. Desperate to keep his condition a secret, he enlists Lord Salisbury to hoodwink the queen into believing he is suffering from a minor ailment. Things take a more worrying turn when Churchill asks Eden to meet the US Secretary of State in his place, only to have the foreign secretary reliance on narcotics and chronic pain send him to a US hospital.

At long last, the all-powerful Tommy Lascelles is ready to retire, but in one last show of influence, he undermines Elizabeth's choice of Martin Charteris as his replacement in favour of his own candidate, Michael Adeane. Tired of being outplayed by the men around her, Her Majesty engages a private tutor to fill in the gaps in her education and emerges ready to read the riot act to Churchill and Salisbury.

The Truth

First things first… during the opening flashback to 1940, Lancasters soar over Windsor Castle. Two years before Lancs were soaring anywhere. But still.

And so to Anthony Eden, *The Crown*'s very own Wile E Coyote, forever trying to oust his nemesis, Winston Churchill. Eden, a formidable foreign secretary during World War Two, gets a rough ride from Peter Morgan and *Scientia Potentia Est* really goes to town on the admittedly fraught relationship between the prime minister and his deputy. This episode shows the fallout as Churchill and Eden find themselves incapacitated at the same time; this much is true. The devil, as they say, is in the details.

Churchill was laid low by his fourth stroke on 23 June 1953, an attack that left him convalescing for four months. Whilst *The Crown* depicts Churchill doing his best to hide the serious nature of his condition from the queen, in reality his poor health was a matter of public knowledge. No effort was made to hoodwink Elizabeth either by his private secretary, Jack Colville, nor the Chancellor of the Exchequer, Richard Austen Butler, who assumed much of the responsibility of the PM's role when Deputy Prime Minister Anthony Eden's collapse put him out of action at this critical time. Poor old Rab Butler, however, doesn't even merit a cameo in this episode despite his vital importance in the real story. Though we have no Butler, we instead get a lot of Lord Salisbury, aka Bobbety, whose scheming to hide Churchill's ill health leads the queen to tut, "never trust a Cecil". This was indeed said of the family, but not until many years later when Bobbety's grandson, Viscount Cranborne, left William Hague high and dry to strike a clandestine deal with Tony Blair.

But we're a long way from Tony Blair at the moment.

In *Scientia Potentia Est*, the nature of the foreign secretary's collapse is somewhat woolly, dramatic though its depiction is. Eden is shown in agonised spasms as he travels from England to America for urgent talks with Secretary of State, John Foster Dulles, even going so far as to beg his aide to administer an injection of some mysterious, unnamed substance. The net result of all this is Eden's collapse, which is witnessed by an unsympathetic Dulles, who laments the last gasps of empire. In the eyes of the world, Britain is tottering. The next time we see Eden, he is in an American hospital awaiting surgery, but still able to gleefully force Churchill to tell him how vital he is to the government's survival. In effect though, the episode tells us that at this tense time when the Soviets were conducting atom bomb tests, the nation had no political leadership at all.

That's not quite how things went.

Anthony Eden had suffered through a series of health crises, but the most serious came in 1953, when his bile duct was damaged during an operation. Complications from this damage left Eden battling an infection which sent him to hospital in the UK and required further corrective surgery. Eden wished for these corrective procedures to be carried out by a particular specialist, Dr Richard Cattell of the Lahey Clinic, Boston. Luckily, Dr Cattell was in London – Eden didn't collapse in the US - and was willing to perform the operations, but only with his own team at his own facility in America. Though Churchill argued for the procedure to take place in London in order to minimise disruption, Cattell wouldn't be moved and Eden travelled to Boston, where he underwent surgery. During his recovery, the foreign secretary was prescribed Benzedrine and other prescription medications, which it's since been theorised may have played a part in many of the poor decisions he made during his own premiership.

All of this, of course, is considerably less dramatic than *The Crown* would have viewers believe. Whilst much has been written about Eden's depression and his reliance on pain killers and prescription narcotics to control his chronic pain, there is no evidence that he ever had members of his staff administer injections. Despite Eden's ongoing feud with Dulles in the 1950s, nor did he fall asleep in front of the Secretary of State with a tell-tale blood spot on his pristine white shirt. Anthony Eden, clothes horse extraordinaire, would never have committed such a sartorial faux pas.

Timeline-wise, there is a little rejigging here too. Churchill had been lobbying for a summit to discuss the matter of Soviet nuclear tests even before the coronation: the meeting eventually happened in Bermuda that December. Eden's spectacular fall from grace will be covered in a later episode but this was one of those might-have-been moments in political history. If Eden had been in good health when Churchill fell ill, as deputy he would have taken over the top job, at least temporarily. Had that happened, the future for Anthony Eden might have turned out very differently.

Politicians aside, the episode has two other main threads. The first is the queen's awareness of her lack of formal education, which in *Scientia Potentia Est* becomes so acute that she enlists the help of the venerable, fictional Professor Hogg to bring her up to intellectual speed. Like Venetia Scott, this is entirely make believe; Professor Hogg is a creation of the scriptwriter designed to show Her Majesty's growing confidence with the role she has inherited. On a related note, when the professor discusses the Military Industrial Complex, he's using a phrase that wasn't coined until 1961. Very forward thinking indeed. The queen did, however, receive some lessons in constitutional history at Eton from vice provost Henry Marten in 1938, as depicted earlier in this episode.

The second thread is the matter of who will succeed Tommy Lascelles as the monarch's Private Secretary. We've already seen a similar succession storyline come up and, once again, this is a matter of drama over accuracy. In *The Crown*, the queen is keen for Martin Charteris, who served as her secretary when she was a princess, to take the job, but Lascelles overrules her to secure the succession of his immediate deputy, Michael Adeane. In reality, the succession of the Private Secretary is virtually a matter of accepted palace routine; Adeane and Lascelles had no need to scheme against Charteris, because he would never have expected to jump ahead of Adeane and assume the role. Just as monarchs enjoy a line of succession, so too do their secretaries. Charteris served as Adeane's deputy until his own turn came.

Incidentally, Charteris's tree-hating wife in *The Crown* has had a change of name. Christened Mary Gay, she always went by her second name; the series refers to her by the first.

Finally, this episode caused some consternation thanks to a suggestion that the queen may, at one time or another, have gone down on her knees in front of her husband. If you follow. Since the couple had four children, I think it's safe to assume that they did more than shake hands, whatever the occasional outraged viewer might have wished was true!

1.8 Pride & Joy

The Crown

Still smarting from the loss of Townsend, Margaret takes full advantage of her sister's absence on a Commonwealth tour to play at being queen herself. To her dismay, her popularity brings Churchill to the palace with a warning that she simply has far too much personality to take Elizabeth's place. With the Queen Mother away in Scotland looking to buy a castle to which she can retreat, Margaret feels more alone than ever.

Meanwhile, the feuding queen and Duke of Edinburgh are embarrassed when they accidentally treat journalists to a front row seat at their marital spat.

The Truth

The timeline is massaged once more in this episode, to the degree that it's really pointless trying to reconcile it with reality. The events depicted in *Pride & Joy* were scattered throughout the first half of the fifties, but in *The Crown*, it's all wrapped up in a few months.

Queen Elizabeth The Queen Mother is feeling blue. She misses her husband, misses her purpose and needs to spend some time by herself, so off she gads to Scotland to buy herself the Castle of Mey as her daughter and son-in-law undertake their official Commonwealth tour. In actuality, the Queen Mother bought the castle in 1952, whereas the couple undertook their tour the following year. It's a small detail, but this blurring of the times is clearly intended to show how much like a spare part the Queen Mother now feels. Elizabeth is a confident and respected queen, and her mother's guiding hand is no longer required. The Queen Mother is so glum that she asks Margaret to assume a central role whilst the queen is absent, as she feels unable to perform her official duties.

This is drama, so we need a reason for the Queen Mother to have some teary scenes and we also need a motive for Margaret to step even further into the limelight, but it's not how things went down. After briefly considering retirement, the Queen Mother listened to the advice of Churchill and decided instead to stay on. She happily carried out her duties as the senior Counsellor of State whilst the Commonwealth tour was underway, as well as caring for young Charles and Anne and meeting regularly with Winston Churchill: she certainly didn't flee to Scotland and leave Margaret with the responsibility of covering for the absent monarch. As a further nod to the tortured timeline, in *Pride & Joy* the Queen Mother's sense that she is becoming redundant really takes hold as she sadly unveils a statue of her late husband. It's a touching emotional moment, except the George VI memorial wasn't unveiled until 1955, long after the Commonwealth tour had been concluded.

Ah well. Anyway, Royal fashion fans should enjoy this episode: there's a fleeting appearance by the queen's legendary dress designer, Sir Norman Hartnell, and we get to see Her Majesty selecting the frocks she'll wear to dazzle her subjects. Though she's reticent to put on too much of a show, Hartnell won't hear of anything else – a show is what the people want. More than any other designer, Sir Norman Hartnell was responsible for the queen's identity in dress. Hartnell received first a Royal Warrant as Dressmaker to Queen Elizabeth (later the Queen Mother) in 1940 and a subsequent Royal Warrant as Dressmaker to Queen Elizabeth II in 1957. Hartnell dressed the queen for her wedding and her coronation, as well as innumerable other glittering occasions throughout her reign.

King George VI described Elizabeth as his pride and Margaret as his joy and, despite her temperamental nature, people certainly did warm to Margaret's vivacious personality and easy command of the limelight. In *Pride & Joy*, this results in Churchill telling her that she must reduce her activities, lest her vivacity show up how dull her sister really is. Martin Charteris, who follows Margaret around during her escapades with a look of impatient concern on his face, would have been unable to do so simply because he was also on the royal tour with Elizabeth and Philip. That would've been a heck of a bus fare to Calverton colliery. Though it's a handy demonstration of the difference in personality between the warring siblings, Margaret actually represented the royal family on multiple occasions after *Pride & Joy* has her being forbidden from ever doing so again. Most notable was her sensational tour of the Caribbean in 1955, where she was received like a superstar.

But it's not all make believe.

One of the scenes that might appear to be fictional comes when Philip and Elizabeth have a furious argument without realising that the press are observing the whole thing. Though today the royal family's every frown is dissected in the media, at the time nobody would have expected to witness an unguarded moment such as this. Yet this really did happen: a moment of discord between the royal couple was observed and palace aides stepped in to ensure it didn't make it as far as the headlines.

During the Victoria leg of the royal tour, journalists were stunned to see Philip storm out of the villa the couple were sharing, only for the queen to follow him, bellowing for him to come back to the house. She grabbed him and yanked him back inside, leaving press secretary Richard Colville to charm cameraman Frank Bagnall into handing over the footage he had captured of the spat. Today, that footage would be on sale to the highest bidder, but Bagnall honourably agreed to expose the film and prevent it from ever being seen. It's a rare moment of accuracy in a generally rather fast and loose episode.

1.9 Assassins

The Crown

Queen Elizabeth II and the Duke of Edinburgh are leading increasingly separate lives, and Her Majesty falls back on the easy-going company of her friend, Porchey. In Parliament, all eyes are turned on Churchill as he prepares to celebrate his 80th birthday, a milestone that will be marked by a portrait commissioned from artist Graham Sutherland. However, when the portrait is unveiled, it depicts an elderly and forlorn figure, leaving the PM outraged.

Facing his increasing age and worsening health, Churchill at last steps down in favour of Anthony Eden, as Clementine has the offending portrait burned.

The Truth

And so, we reach the penultimate episode of the first season, and there's trouble at t'mill, as Elizabeth and Philip as clashing. Again. But that's really par for the course by now.

With things at home ever more tense, the queen seeks a distraction in the company of her beloved old friend, Lord Porchester, aka Porchey. Lord Porchester was Henry Herbert 7th Earl of Carnarvon, and he and the queen had been close since they were teenagers. In adulthood, Porchey managed the royal racing stables and was one of just two people to have Her Majesty's personal mobile phone number in later years – the other was Princess Anne. Although there's no doubt that the couple were close confidantes, *The Crown* imbues their relationship with a rather more rueful, romantic air. Constantly battling with the Duke of Edinburgh, the hint is that Her Majesty's friends and family had once expected that she would marry Porchey and that she wished she had done so, thus incurring Philip's jealousy and vitriol when she starts spending more and more time with her reliable old pal. There's no evidence of that: they really were just good friends.

The second theme of this penultimate episode comes courtesy of the aging, ailing Winston Churchill. He is approaching his 80th birthday, which means it must be November 1954. Facing pressure to step aside in favour of the younger, smoother Anthony Eden, it is a contemplative prime minister who agrees to sit for a portrait celebrating his remarkable life and career. Artist Graham Sutherland comes to Chartwell to work on the portrait, as Churchill reflects on his own artistic ambitions, as well as his mortality. Sadly, the story Churchill tells of his daughter's death is true: Marigold fell victim to septicaemia in 1921, at the age of two.

Just as *Assassins* shows, the former prime minister remained a devoted painter throughout his life and loved to indulge his passion for art at Chartwell, his beloved country estate. Chartwell, Churchill's sanctuary, loomed large in the statesman's life, just as it does in this episode. It is here that, in *Assassins,* Anthony Eden arrives to berate his friend and rival. Furious and hysterical in equal measure, he demands that Churchill step aside. The clear indication is that Eden is a man on the edge and one who, whether through stress, ill health or prescription medication, is barely fit to lead. The timeline goes askew here again, as Eden rants at Churchill about the latter's health crisis two months earlier. Yet since we saw that health crisis on screen, a six-month tour of the Commonwealth has been depicted... either the foreign secretary's painkillers have affected his memory, or Peter Morgan has got his dates mixed up.

Either way, it's worth noting that whilst we have no record of the two men ever having such a bitter argument over who was more likely to drop down dead first, Eden did have a furiously hot temper. A micromanager with a hare trigger temperament, Eden could flip from serenity to fury in the blink of an eye, as *Assassins* is all too keen to demonstrate. There's likewise no doubt that he found the long wait for Churchill's resignation frustrating, as anyone would.

When Sutherland's painting is unveiled at a prestigious ceremony in Westminster Hall, Churchill is horrified. Rather than the depiction of an elder statesman that he was hoping for, he sees a portrait of a scowling, belligerent and pathetic old man. The ceremony that marked the unveiling was televised by the BBC and though Churchill's speech is massaged to make it a little more pointed, the real speech he gave was similar in tone and content to the one he speaks here. In addition, Churchill's reaction to the portrait in *Assassins* is indeed accurate, though the painting has been edited somewhat from the studies that still exist of the original. He loathed the work and, just as Morgan's script posits, really was denied the right to see the work in progress by the intensely private Sutherland. The depiction of Churchill's first view of the work is fictionalised, however, as he got his initial glimpse of it in a photograph given to him by his wife Clementine, rather than cold during the televised ceremony as Anthony Eden looks on with malicious amusement.

Within days of receiving Sutherland's painting, the prime minister has made up his mind. He lumbers along to see the queen and hands over his resignation, keeping his word and passing the crown to Anthony Eden as he leaves high office behind. As Churchill leaves the palace, Eden arrives. The rivals shake hands and the torch is officially passed. Though it's an effective way to show the changing of the guard, Churchill didn't leave office immediately after the painting was unveiled: he stuck around for another five months. Anthony Eden made his longed-for succession to the top job in April 1955; by mid-January 1957, it was all over.

The fate of Graham Sutherland's painting was unknown until the passing of Lady Churchill, but *Assassins* sort of gets it right. Just as

Clementine previously destroyed portraits of her husband that she disliked, so too did that fate befall Sutherland's work. A year or so after Sutherland's painting was unveiled, Clementine had it taken to a remote location by a member of her private secretary's family. There it was cut into pieces and burned. Naturally, *The Crown* shows Lady Churchill watching over the inferno herself, just days after her husband's retirement. As the first season approaches its final act, going up in flames – both literally and symbolically - appears to be the order of the day.

1.10 Gloriana

The Crown

Margaret and Townsend are back with a vengeance and their romance has split the country down the middle, leaving the public on one side and a disapproving Parliament and Church on the other. Elizabeth is forced to take decisive action and she forbids the marriage once and for all, leaving Townsend with no choice but to depart for his new posting in Brussels.

Though things are a little less rocky between the royal couple, Philip's increasingly overbearing attitude towards Prince Charles is becoming a problem. To get him out of the way and give both husband and wife some breathing space, Lascelles suggests that the duke should open the Summer Olympics in Australia.

In Downing Street, Prime Minister Anthony Eden finds that the prize he has coveted for so long is the proverbial poisoned chalice. As the British dispute with Egypt's President Nasser spirals out of control, he turns once more to medication for relief.

The Truth

And so it's curtains for the star-crossed lovers at last. As Princess Margaret finally passes the magical milestone of her 25th birthday, she is freed from the restrictions of the Royal Marriages Act and can, should she desire, submit her request to marry Group Captain Peter Townsend to Parliament and the Privy Council for consent. The couple are still in love and the queen, released from the need to consent to the marriage, is happy to throw her support behind Margaret's blissful dreams of a fairy-tale wedding. Unfortunately, nobody told Margaret that she still had to jump through hoops with Parliament before the wedding could take place; they'd simply been hoping that she'd lose interest in the two years since Townsend was packed off to Brussels.

One of the themes that will develop over the next few seasons is that of the testy relationship between the Duke of Edinburgh and his eldest son, Prince Charles. We've already seen Philip lambasting his lad for not being a football fan and now, as they fish together, things are tense again. There is some truth in this, as we now know that relations between the duke and the prince weren't always rosy. Philip, outdoorsy, athletic and one of the boys, was a very different sort of chap to the bookish Prince Charles, who was more at home in the greenhouse than on the football field. Polo, of course, was a different matter. *The Crown* will really go to town on the theme of a father and son who seem to be speaking two different languages in later seasons, but the foundations are definitely laid here.

The Queen Mother and Tommy Lascelles decide that Philip should be sent to Australia to officially open the Summer Olympics, so plans are afoot to make sure he arrives in time for the opening ceremony in November. There's just one problem: Margaret and Townsend split in 1955, whereas the Olympic Games took place in November 1956. The Duke of Edinburgh won't arrive on time in *The Crown*'s universe, but a full twelve months early. He'll be there before the torch is even lit.

As perceived free spirited outsiders from the family, Margaret and Philip begin to build a rapport built on mutual dissatisfaction. It's the stuff of drama alright, but it's also a little disingenuous. Despite Margaret's unhappy love life, she was far from an outsider: in fact, her Caribbean tour of 1955 had been a huge hit and she was very definitely one of the royal in-crowd. Likewise, whilst *The Crown* has shown us the Duke of Edinburgh's dissatisfaction in what seems like every episode, the suggestion that he was bundled off to Australia to get him out of the way is inaccurate. Philip was just doing his duty.

After waiting in the wings for so long to get hold of the keys to Downing Street, it's true that Anthony Eden soon discovered that the job wasn't all it was cracked up to be. The series laid the groundwork for unrest in Egypt in a previous episode and, as the Edens arrive at Balmoral – Mrs Eden still decorous and silent, her husband still popping painkillers like they're going out of style – the situation is growing more dire. Season two will take us to North Africa and the spectacular downfall of Anthony Eden, but once again the foundations are going down for future storylines. Also note the paparazzi who pursue Townsend until he narrowly avoids a car accident: the parallels with Diana's storyline are hardly accidental.

In scenes depicting Eden and the queen's discussions of Margaret's relationship, the scriptwriters have once again set aside truth in favour of romantic drama. Elizabeth is torn between her sister and her duty. It is a conflict that she will encounter time and again, but here she is faced with what seems like an impossible choice: uphold protocol and break her sister's heart, or support Margaret and put sibling loyalty over duty. She needs some advice and turns to a very unlikely agony uncle indeed: the abdicated king.

When dispensing wisdom to the queen, the Duke of Windsor is once again in erudite form, advising his niece on what it means to be a monarch and a human. And for some reason, his pearls of wisdom become the cornerstone of Elizabeth's transformation from sister to sovereign. She must protect the crown and the kingdom, even if it means betraying her sibling. Frankly, the thought of Her Majesty taking advice on life as a monarch from her abdicated uncle is close to absurd, but the issue is one of show don't tell. It's tough to show someone simply thinking through a difficult choice, but giving a contentious character some meaningful lines that we can watch Elizabeth react to serves its purpose.

In *Gloriana*, Morgan posits that Margaret and Townsend were being forced down the Edward and Mrs Simpson route, as the unsympathetic PM informs Her Majesty that, if the wedding is to go ahead, Princess Margaret must renounce her rank and privileges, marry overseas and live abroad on a limited budget until the drama blows over. After much back and forth with Eden and the church, Elizabeth tells Margaret that she can have Townsend or her family; she cannot have both. The suggestion is that it was a heinous and painful act of betrayal, as Elizabeth turns her back on her sister in order to satisfy her role as queen.

This is make believe.

In reality, Anthony Eden had no objection to the marriage at all; as a divorcee who had faced a storm of criticism for remarrying, he was sympathetic to the couple's plight and saw no reason why Townsend's previous marriage nor his social standing should be a barrier to the union. He and the queen put their heads together to draw up a plan that would allow the couple to wed on the stipulation that Princess Margaret would surrender both her right of succession and that of any children she might have with Townsend. In return for that sacrifice, she would retain her titles, privileges and rank. Since Margaret's succession would require the deaths of not only the queen, but all her children too, it seemed like a done deal.

Ultimately, despite *The Crown*'s assertion that Elizabeth forced her sister to give up her one chance of happiness and essentially ruined her life, the decision was Margaret's. When it came to the crunch, she chose to retain her place in the line of succession over taking the plunge with Peter Townsend. She reached her decision after long conversations with her mother, both in letters and, we assume, in person. Yet in *The Crown*, the Queen Mother is entirely absent from the debate, which is really stretching credibility. Either way, the end of the affair was certainly not due to the queen's interference, nor Anthony Eden's disapproval.

But in our fictional world, Margaret and Townsend split not because Margaret won't surrender her right of succession, but because she cannot bring herself to be cut from the family as the Duke of Windsor was. After a tearful goodbye, the broken-hearted Group Captain composes and delivers a speech to the waiting press. In it, he explains that Margaret's faith would not have allowed her to marry a divorcee. It is presented as Townend's statement and Townsend's statement alone; needless to say, it wasn't. This speech was actually a jointly written statement issued by Princess Margaret: Townsend neither gave nor would have expected to give a press conference. It simply wasn't done. It's a misstep in a series that has too often turned the spotlight on men at pivotal moments when the perspective of the female participants remains ignored.

Furthermore, whilst it's true that the statement was worked on by both Margaret and Townsend, it was issued in her name alone; by putting the words in Townsend's mouth, Margaret is denied a voice. Whilst perhaps this isn't as literal as the infuriatingly silent Clarissa Eden, Margaret's silence is one of the most frustrating things about season one and this is a scene in which she should have spoken. It goes hand in hand with Margaret's curious description of herself as unhinged; though she was mercurial, and apparently could be spiteful and hot tempered, *unhinged* feels like a step too far. In a series that has been dominated by male characters, Margaret has certainly been dealt a bad hand with this particular line of dialogue.

Oh, and that precredit sequence? Wallis was in France at the time, which would've made meaningful dances with her paramour a little difficult.

For prime minister Eden, the storm clouds are gathering. A self-administered injection of painkillers leaves him insensible as a film of Nasser railing against the British literally burns on the screen behind him. Foreshadowing is in full force here, with Philip speeding away from Buckingham Palace, President Nasser of Egypt towering over Anthony Eden and the queen, stone-faced and magnificent, being lauded by Cecil Beaton and enshrined by the lens of his camera. As Beaton tells her, "Gloriana, forgetting Elizabeth Windsor now, now only Elizabeth Regina".

The season ends on the image of Her Majesty Queen Elizabeth II, silent and stoic. She has survived her earliest years as queen and is now, we are told portentously, *Gloriana*.

❊❊SEASON 2❊❊

2.1 Misadventure

The Crown

Is it curtains for the Queen and the Duke of Edinburgh? No, because divorce is not an option. However, with Elizabeth sure that her husband is sleeping with a Russian ballet dancer, things are bleak as Philip departs for his royal tour.

Life isn't much happier at Downing Street, where Anthony Eden is scheming to use the military against Egyptian forces in Suez. When the queen learns of the underhand strategy, Eden admits that the invasion is part of a secret pact between Britain, Israel and France, which will allow Britain to reclaim the Suez Canal without involving the UN or Parliament. Outmanoeuvred, the queen reluctantly gives her consent.

The Truth

Season two drops us straight into February 1957 and, just as it was in real life, the country is rife with speculation about the state of the royal marriage. In fact, just to prove that everything old is new again, in reality the Palace actually issued a statement denying there was any marital strife later that same year. *Misadventure* then tracks back through the months to suggest that the cause of this strife was Philip's attraction to ballet dancer Galina Ulanova, the prima ballerina of the Bolshoi Ballet. This places us in autumn 1956, when Ulanova visited the UK and Philip was about to embark on his royal Commonwealth tour.

Keen *Crown* watchers will detect a slight confusion here, as season one ended in 1955 with Philip preparing to depart for Australia. The timeline has at last caught up to reality and a whole year has passed, thus putting Philip in the right place at the right time. One thing that isn't in the right place, however, is the swift cut to Egypt and the raiding of the Suez Canal offices, which took place in late July, several months before the events of this episode.

Eden learns of Egypt's actions whilst he is giving a rather smug speech to the pupils at Eton College, perhaps in an effort to raise the spectre of 9/11 and George W Bush reading storybooks as the world went up in flames. In fact, Eden was hosting King Faisal II of Iraq at dinner when he received the report, but there's a certain sangfroid in having his own world start to fall apart as he crows about the unique skill Etonians have for leadership.

For a series that has played fast and loose with the truth and conjured up fictional characters where necessary, the decision to use Ulanova's name as Prince Phillip's suggested love interest is certainly an intriguing one. Though rumours of his playboy proclivities were rife, there has never been any proof that the Duke of Edinburgh was unfaithful and he was never linked to Ulanova at all; indeed, they never had an opportunity to meet, let alone become a couple. His name was most often connected to actress Pat Kirkwood, whose legs critic Kenneth Tynan called "the eighth wonder of the world", but it is Ulanova's photograph that the queen finds in her husband's luggage as he leaves for his tour down under. Whither Pat Kirkwood?

It might have made more sense in this case for Morgan to pull another convenient Venetia out of his hat and give us a fictional candidate to catch the duke's eye, because Galina Ulanova certainly didn't. She rarely performed outside the Soviet Union and by the time she made her single visit to London, where the queen saw her dance, Philip was mere days away from leaving for his tour. He and the dancer never met but, on a similar note, one can't help but wince at Margaret's chatter regarding illicit hookups at Philip's Thursday club, where an osteopath (no doubt Stephen Ward, who is coming up this season) is procuring ballerinas for members. As a prima ballerina of the Bolshoi, it's unlikely that Ulanova was being procured for anyone.

Having set up the Suez Crisis as the political opener to this new season, *The Crown* does a fairly good job of communicating the main planks of Anthony Eden's downfall in a relatively limited screen time. In case you found yourself lost in plot and counter plot, what precipitated the crisis was Egyptian President Nasser's seizure and nationalisation of the Suez Canal Company, which was controlled by British and French interests. Fearing that this seizure of power would cut off oil supplies to Europe, Britain, France and Israel secretly joined forces to attempt a disastrous invasion of Egypt in 1956 in an effort to wrest back control. Israel invaded first and shortly after, France and Britain went in to supposedly put an end to the conflict. The trio hoped against hope that the international community would never learn that they had cooked up the plan beforehand. Of course, it didn't go that way.

Faced with condemnation from the United Nations and even the possibility of sanctions, the once popular Eden was forced into a humiliating climbdown, which set the stage for the end of his political career. *The Crown* accurately shows that Eden attempted to cover up his poor decisions by lying to Parliament, the Palace and the UN as protests against him gripped London. This is true; after waiting years to take centre stage, the perennial understudy had blown his one big chance. When his wife, Clarissa, went out to view the protests first-hand, she knew that her husband's days at the top were numbered. The fallout plunged the nation into economic freefall, damaging the special relationship with the United States and cementing the United Kingdom's declining status as a world power.

Just as Eden lurked in the shadows behind Churchill, our lurking politician this season is Chancellor of the Exchequer Harold Macmillan, who is ready to let his PM hang himself and leave the keys to Downing Street in the door. Macmillan's real role in Eden's downfall differs depending on which account one reads, but there's little doubt that the chancellor played the waiting game. He possessed the patience that George VI had recommended to Eden back in season one.

When Elizabeth learns of Eden's plans – though not his duplicity – she disapproves of his decision to invade Egypt without going through the proper channels. Though the queen never discussed her opinions on matters political, Lord Mountbatten claimed that she frowned on of her prime minister's ill thought out handling of Suez and, shortly before his death, Eden admitted that "I would not claim she was pro-Suez.". In *The Crown*, of course, Her Majesty asks Eden outright if Britain has colluded with Israel and he comes clean, scrambling to justify his actions. It is a moment that shows Elizabeth has finally switched on to current affairs. It's not a fiction either, as Eden really did conceal his plans from the queen, largely because he didn't want her publicly embarrassed if it all went belly up. Still, whilst it's nice to know that Elizabeth is finally confident when dealing with the men in suits. Unfortunately, it's undermined by the fact that the monarch only starts to take notice *after* she misses important paperwork because she's too busy mooning over Philip's fancies. It takes a telling off from Mountbatten to bring her attention back to her duties. It's all a bit unnecessary really.

And though we all know that sometimes necessity means there must be a little bit of playing around when it comes to location, as Anthony Eden visits his old alma mater to tell the boys at Eton that they are the future of Great Britain, there's an amusing production blooper. He gets a good laugh from his audience by mocking the very idea that leaders might come from Harrow… in scenes filmed at Harrow. In fact, visible over Eden's shoulder as he mocks the other place are the crests of the very prime ministers who came from Harrow.

Finally, poor old Princess Margaret is once again dealt a dud hand as she's boozing until dawn, sniping at her sister and being generally difficult to live with. All well and good, were it not for the fact that when this episode takes place, she was actually on her own well-received official world tour. But where's the drama in that?

2.2 A Company of Men

The Crown

Having taken a thrashing in Egypt, Eden calls British forces into retreat and flees to Jamaica for some R&R. Philip is also far away, fielding questions about his cloudy family history during his solo tour of the southern hemisphere. Lonely without his wife and children, Philip's loving radio address from Graham Land prompts Elizabeth to include a secret message to him in her Christmas speech.

Though things seem to be back on track for the royal couple, a messy divorce for Philip's private secretary, Michael Parker, sees the courtiers prepare for possible press interest in the Duke of Edinburgh's own marriage.

The Truth

Long regarded as one of the most disastrous prime ministers in modern history, Anthony Eden blotted his remarkable copybook as foreign secretary with his short-lived tenure at Downing Street. Years of poor health had left Eden reliant on a cocktail of prescription drugs to control his pain, drugs that very likely impaired his judgement during the Suez crisis. *A Company of Men* carries dark hints of this, showing the prime minister falling into crisis when no stronger narcotics can be found to replace the pentobarbitone that has ceased to have any effect. Curiously, the bottle is labelled as amphetamine but it's actually the precise opposite: a barbiturate that is used as a sedative, rather than a stimulant.

At this time of the national crisis, Eden's doctors informed him that his life was at risk if he continued in office and suggested that he take a restorative break. His decision to travel to Ian Fleming's Goldeneye estate in Jamaica and entrust the country to Butler and Macmillan may well have done wonders for Eden's health, but it was catastrophic for his premiership. At a time when Britain was in economic freefall, its prime minister was sunning himself on a far-flung beach with the man behind James Bond. Though he survived a vote of no confidence in November, Eden's political career never recovered from the outcry: his days were numbered. Given the Bond connection as Clarissa Eden was godmother to the Flemings' son and Eden's security staff carved welcome messages on the trees at Goldeneye, much to the author's annoyance, it seems curious that there was no cameo appearance for the creator of 007 in *The Crown*.

Away from Downing Street, Philip is boorishly meeting the locals on his Commonwealth tour aboard Britannia, whilst Eileen Parker, neglected wife of his secretary, Mike, is looking for evidence that will support her divorce case. Against a montage of Philip having a little bit too much fun, society photographer and club founder Baron Narhum reads a letter from Parker aloud to the denizens of the Thursday Club. The fictional letter is the very essence of lads on tour and Baron reads it with just the right amount of lasciviousness, but there's just one problem: a month before Philip left to undertake his tour, Baron died following surgery. And yet here he is, merrily reading a mucky letter two months or so after his own death.

Eileen Parker did indeed seek a separation from her husband, a scandal that turned the media spotlight on the royal marriage and staff relations inside the palace. In her 1982 tell-all book, *Step Aside for Royalty*, the former Mrs Parker hinted that her husband was unfaithful, but held back from making specific allegations. Instead, she described a marriage that crumbled under the strain of her husband's demanding career. If she undertook any of the sleuthing we see on screen in order to uncover her spouse's infidelity, she chose not to disclose it.

Anyway, whilst the ghost of Baron is raising raucous laughs in London, in Australia, Philip is making eyes at fictional reporter Helen King, but she isn't interested in the duke's flirty ways. Instead, she's our gateway to a flashback regarding the mental breakdown and subsequent hospitalisation of Philip's mother, as well as his father's frequent absences. There's truth to both facets of Philip's life and Helen King's comments regarding his life in Germany, the death of his favourite sister and his siblings' closeness to the Nazi high command are accurate to varying degrees. We'll hear lots more about all of this and examine these varying degrees in episodes to come.

Once again, this is a Philip-heavy episode. As the duke struggles with his role and his unhappy memories, he is able to make himself useful by saving a shipwrecked fisherman despite the disapproval of Britannia's captain and insists that they take an expensive detour to return him to his homeland. So far, so heroic. So fictional. Though Philip did rescue the two-man crew of a bomber that had ditched in the Pacific in 1945, the episode depicted in *The Crown* didn't happen; Philip's royal tour was uneventful and unmarked by clashes with the master of Britannia. He certainly wouldn't have dismissed Vice-Admiral Sir Conolly Abel Smith as a man who sat out World War II either: naval man Philip would have known that Smith served with distinction in both World Wars and wouldn't have dreamed of treating his superior officer with anything other than due respect and deference.

In the closing act of the episode, both the Duke of Edinburgh and the queen make speeches which contain secret messages of love for their each other and their children. Whilst the speeches themselves are fictionalised, the couple did indeed both make a Christmas speech in 1957, though Philip's was a relatively brief message versus that delivered by his wife.

And one last thing: Philip's fake beard really is a shocker.

2.3 Lisbon

The Crown

Eden returns to England to face protests from the public and Parliament alike in the wake of disastrous Suez crisis. After a scant time at the top, he is forced to stand down in favour of Harold Macmillan.

Michael Adeane and Tommy Lascelles do their best to convince Eileen Parker not to proceed with her divorce. Though they even enlist the help of the queen to keep the marriage together, their efforts are to no avail. With press speculation growing ever more feverish, Parker is forced to resign as the Queen and Duke face make or break talks about their future.

The Truth

Whilst it's always a treat to see Tommy Lascelles back in the saddle, to see him back as the scheming Machiavelli that Peter Morgan seems so determined to depict is such a missed opportunity. What a pleasure it would be to see some reflection of the pragmatic, good-humoured and empathetic figure Lascelles seems to have been in reality.

After a little bit of R&R in Jamaica, Mr Eden is back to find that a country that once adored him no longer wants him at the helm. Eden had run out of fight and his departure for the West Indies left the British people feeling abandoned and the cabinet looking for a candidate to replace their tarnished leader. Once again, how the fateful cabinet meeting went down is dependent on who you believe; whilst it's generally agreed that Macmillan did turn his back on the PM and make a grab for power, there were a few differing recollections as to how it happened. Macmillan's son recalled that his father had intended not to lead, but to retire, whereas Clarissa Eden wrote that there were a good many tears and a fair bit of temper before her husband accepted the inevitable.

After a bitter tirade against the betrayal of his colleagues, the weeping PM had to leave the room to compose himself. On his return, he had accepted his fate. As the script reflects, Eden officially left office due to concerns for his health, as opposed to his catastrophic performance in the top job. It was an expedient and face-saving excuse that gave him the get out he needed, but it was true: the work had nearly killed him.

The timeline is all over the place again, as we see the Edens arriving back in England after Christmas and making a flying visit to Sandringham where the prime minister will tender his resignation. In fact, they arrived home in mid-December and spent the night at Sandringham on 8 January. Anthony Eden officially resigned on the evening of 9 January at Buckingham Palace.

What is intriguing, given the series' love of political wheeling and dealing, is the fact that Morgan chose not to dramatise how Macmillan rose to the premiership. Eden's pick was his deputy, Leader of the House Rab Butler, an appointment which the press also expected, whilst the party was split between Butler and Macmillan. Though the queen had no vote, she sought advice from Churchill, who preferred Macmillan as the better candidate. Macmillan agreed and had held a series of secret meetings with his cabinet colleagues and even President Eisenhower, all of whom he assured would be properly taken care of should he come to power. When the cabinet voted in secret, Macmillan clinched the victory. And so it was decided.

Which leaves Harold Macmillan as the next Tory lamb to the slaughter and the last gasp of a dying political breed. If he thinks he can get one over on Her Majesty, though, he's in for a surprise. After voicing her sympathy and understanding to the departing Eden, Elizabeth is ready to tell Macmillan some home truths, reminding Supermac that, as chancellor, he was a loud voice in support of Anthony Eden's decisions regarding Suez. The young woman who could once be cajoled and bullied by the politicians has learned a thing or two.

And so it's back to the Parkers, and this episode really takes the facts and ties them into a big old complicated fictional bow. In reality, Eileen Parker hoped to keep her separation private, but her lawyer issued a public statement whilst her husband was away on the royal tour. Though the queen and Duke of Edinburgh both tried to convince Parker not to resign, he chose to do so as a result of the media furore that erupted. In fact, so fevered was the speculation about the royal marriage in light of the Parkers' split that the Palace issued a statement of its own, denying any rift between Elizabeth and Philip.

The Crown plays things a little differently. Though Parker actually remained in Philip's service for some time after his separation became public knowledge, *Lisbon* shows an angry Philip dismiss Parker from his service whilst on board the Britannia. The crux of the matter is the letter that the ghost of Baron Narhum read out, a letter that didn't exist in reality. If that wasn't dramatic enough, the queen actually undertakes a secret mission to convince Eileen to change her mind and stay true to her husband. It goes without saying that such a mission never took place: Her Majesty didn't arrive incognito to do a little bit of impromptu marriage counselling and Tommy Lascelles had no part to play in any element of the eventual Parker divorce. On the plus side, this story has brought the little-seen Queen Mother back to the screen, albeit a version of the Queen Mother who doesn't know where Baltimore is, despite the loathed Wallis Simpson having been one of its most famous citizens.

The Philip show continues as the Duke of Edinburgh finally returns home after months away on his Commonwealth tour and, naturally, he's still feeling hard done to for no specific reason. Whilst it's a frosty reception for the on-screen duke, in reality when he and Elizabeth were happily reunited in Lisbon he found his merry wife and the welcoming party all wearing fake ginger beards; what speculation there had been about the marriage was silenced.

The Crown is very keen to play up the duke's dissatisfaction with his lot for the sake of drama and today's source of malcontent is Philip's jealousy towards his own son, Prince Charles. In *Lisbon*, Philip demands that he be made a Prince of the United Kingdom to assuage his dissatisfaction, whereas the honour was actually bestowed as thanks for his service on his Commonwealth tour. He had been born a prince and had rescinded the title when he married, so to restore it was a move that made perfect sense, as well as sending a message of gratitude for his service to his adopted nation. Churchill had originally suggested this happen in 1955, but the duke declined; Macmillan reiterated the request in 1957 and it was accepted.

This imaginary mini-coronation ceremony makes for an odd scene, with a jubilant and rather villainous duke sitting on his throne looking as though he's about to take over the world, and the queen apparently anything but happy about this turn of events. All in all, a bit of a strange one, capped off by the queen requesting that Michael Adeane shave off his moustache in response to her husband's complaint about the "moustaches" who run things. You probably don't need me to tell you that this is very definitely fiction.

2.4 Beryl

The Crown

Searching for something to take her mind off the absence of Peter Townsend, Margaret accepts a proposal from her friend, Billy Wallace, only to break off the engagement after her paramour takes part in an ill-advised duel.

During a fateful and awkward social gathering, Margaret meets society photographer Antony Armstrong-Jones, and agrees to a photographic sitting. The resultant portrait, in which the princess appears to be nude, causes a scandal that delights Margaret. Things are rocky at Downing Street, where Macmillan's wife refuses to end a long-term affair that has come between the couple.

The Truth

With Philip presumably happy for a little while, the spotlight of angst this episode is turned on Princess Margaret. We haven't seen much of Margaret since she and Peter Townsend parted, but that's all about to change, because Margaret is on the road to love. In *Beryl*, the princess encounters society photographer Antony Armstrong-Jones as he takes photos at the wedding of her lady-in-waiting, Lady Anne Coke. So far, so accurate, though whether the princess was really in such a glowering mood when she first laid eyes on him is a little more questionable. Also questionable is the frankly gothic turn Margaret has taken since Townsend left England, throwing herself around her bedroom in a drunken mania and lurching violently from spite to booze bottle with barely a second to inhale her ciggie. It's another episode where it might have been nice to see and hear a little more of the real Margaret. But she is, for better or worse, a cypher in *The Crown*.

Margaret surrounded herself with admirers as she nursed her broken heart and one of the most loyal was her childhood friend, socialite Billy Wallace. Wallace was a familiar figure at the side of the princess and there had long been rumours that Billy and Margaret might well tie the knot. In *The Crown*, the couple agree to marry simply because they're the only single members of their social set left; though it might seem stranger than fiction, it happened. In 1956, after several playful proposals from Wallace, Margaret said yes.

The timeline in *Beryl* is particularly tortured, bringing together as it does the October 1957 Sputnik launch, the queen's 10th wedding anniversary the following month, a photoshoot from 1950 and a proposal from 1956. Such things are par for the course. Margaret intends to announce her engagement at the queen's 10th wedding anniversary dinner but is prevented from doing so when Wallace is injured in a duel with Colin Tennant, another of the princess's paramours. Though it's perfectly in keeping with the louche Drones Club set that Margaret runs with, this is an invention of the scriptwriters. The actual engagement ended when Billy got intimate with a woman during a trip to the Bahamas; he confessed to Margaret and she dropped him like a hot brick. In the show, Margaret walks out of the 1957 anniversary banquet as her sister is receiving rapturous applause. In fact, she didn't attend at all. Instead, much to the consternation of the press, Princess Margaret went to see a show then on to dinner, only returning to Buckingham Palace when it was time to join the dancing.

There are a couple of things in this episode, however, that *The Crown* gets very right. The first is the ongoing marital discord between Harold and Dorothy Macmillan, largely thanks to an affair with Robert Boothby which lasted more than three decades. Macmillan was tortured by the relationship and wrongly suspected that his daughter might actually be Boothby's child. Though the series doesn't dig too deeply into the unhappy Macmillan marriage, when it does so, it portrays things as they were.

The other accurate depiction is of the fateful introduction of Tony and Margaret at a dinner party given by her lady-in-waiting, Lady Elizabeth Cavendish. In an effort to cheer up her royal friend, Lady Elizabeth invited her to meet all her bohemian pals; it had not been a serious attempt at matchmaking, but Margaret and Armstrong-Jones began their affair soon after. The scenes of their photographic sessions and Tony making Margaret wait in his studio also have foundations in reality, as do the mirror Tony has his subjects sign with a diamond and the motorcycle rides the couple take through the London night.

Where fact and fiction part company is in the scandalous and apparently topless photo of Margaret that she and Tony send to newspapers across the world, causing a furore that *really* upsets the queen. The photo in *Beryl* is an amalgamation of two pictures, one of which was taken in 1959 and one in 1967. By the 1959 sitting Armstrong-Jones had already photographed the queen and by 1967 he was her brother-in-law. The earlier image of Margaret was her official birthday portrait and though both portraits raised eyebrows due to their unconventional nature, the show's suggestion that the princess and photographer conspired to cause a massive scandal and upset her family more than ever before is a fiction. The real scandal was yet to come.

2.5 Marionettes

The Crown

After Elizabeth gives a tone-deaf speech at a car plant, Lord Altrincham attacks the queen's stilted manner and haughty ways in a newspaper article. When public opinion turns against her, Her Majesty seeks to prove her modernising credentials by giving her first televised Christmas address. The groundbreaking move doesn't go down well with the family.

The Truth

In *Marionettes*, *The Crown* turns its attention back to the historical record via a hairdressing detour that neatly spoofs the coronation of Elizabeth II.

In August 1957 the queen was attacked by John Grigg, 2nd Baron Altrincham, a title he would eventually surrender, as priggish and out of touch. In an article for *The National and Evening Review*, entitled *The Monarchy Today*, Lord Altrincham criticised not only Her Majesty's personality and manner of speaking, but also the way in which the Palace was run, suggesting it was a relic of an out of touch world. The public responded to his attack with righteous indignation, though they snapped up copies of the newspapers which ran Lord Altrincham's article on the monarchy in their droves. *The Crown* posits that the touchpaper was lit by a speech the queen gave at a Jaguar factory; this, however, is wrong.

Though she did visit a Jaguar factory in 1956, almost eighteen months before Altrincham's article was published, no such speech was made, whether good, bad or indifferent.

When the article was published, thousands of letters of support for the queen poured in. Though many of them attacked Baron Altrincham for his perceived anti-monarchist views, he was nothing of the sort. None were more indignant that Philip Kinghorn Burbidge, a man with far-right sympathies who punched Altrincham in the face in retribution for his attack on the sovereign. Burbidge was a member of the extreme League of Empire Loyalists and his attack earned him a 20-shilling fine, but the Palace took notice of the intense debate and called Altrincham in.

Whilst *The Crown* shows him attending a meeting with Martin Charteris, the queen's assistant private secretary, only to find Elizabeth herself waiting for him, in reality, the meeting was only with Charteris. Her Majesty stayed away. Charteris and Altrincham discussed the criticisms made in the article and, it seems, the royal household took them on board. Though Baron Altrincham didn't personally tell the queen to televise the Christmas message, nor did he enjoy a private audience with her, Charteris certainly listened to what he had to say. Three decades later, he publicly thanked Altrincham for the service his criticisms did the monarchy.

Just as *The Crown* depicts, Lord Altrincham was interviewed on television by Robin Day and the broadcast gave him a wide platform to air his views, as well as the chance for Burbidge to punch him in the face, but it also struck home in Buckingham Palace. Charteris's personal meeting with Altrincham was testament to his impact. Although there is a good dose of fiction in this episode, it depicts an important watershed in the history of the monarchy: for the first time, though definitely not the last, the sovereign was forced to modernise. It was a theme Peter Morgan had already explored, along with a very meaningful stag, in his earlier movie, *The Queen*.

And for the first time in 1957, the Queen's Christmas message made it onto television sets all over the world: this really had little to do with Altrincham's comments and was something that the woman herself had requested. Whilst Baron Altrincham certainly played his part in bringing the monarchy into the twentieth century, Elizabeth II's role in cementing her own popularity can't be underestimated. Sad to say that

Marionettes takes a reductive view of her efforts and puts the onus once more in the hands of one of the Eton-educated gentlemen who make up the supporting cast.

2.6 Vergangenheit

The Crown

In 1945, a captured German soldier leads American troops to a secret cache of classified documents that had once belonged to Hitler's translator. Having been suppressed by Churchill and George VI for a decade, the papers rear their head again just as the Duke of Windsor stirs the pot in England. Their contents prove disturbing to Elizabeth, who learns that her uncle's connections to Nazi Germany run deeper than she'd suspected.

The Truth

Flashbacks in *The Crown* often herald the appearance of the Duke of Windsor and *Vergangenheit* is no exception. It's also another episode that dips into the historical record with some measure of accuracy… by *Crown* standards, anyway. The crux of *Vergangenheit*, which translates as "the past", is the story of the Marburg Files.

Much of what we see in the opening sequence of this episode is heavily dramatised, but this is a drama, after all. In the dying days of World War II, papers are handed over to American forces by a German soldier who knew that he had in his possession one heck of a scoop. The papers were from the collection of Adolf Hitler's personal translator and revealed that the Duke of Windsor had enjoyed friendly links with senior members of the Nazi regime. With agreement from the palace, Churchill suppressed the papers, hoping to avoid an embarrassing diplomatic incident.

The facts of the Marburg Files are as follows. As American soldiers were travelling through Degenershausen Estate, they found a cache of papers that had been signed by Joachim von Ribbentrop, the Nazi Foreign Minister and rumoured former flame of Wallis Simpson. This discovery led to further searches of Marburg Castle, which in turn coincided with the arrest of Karl von Loesch, who had served as assistant to Paul-Otto Schmidt, the Fuhrer's translator. Against orders from Schmidt, who had commanded that his papers be burned, Loesch had instead buried some of them in the grounds of Marburg Castle. Facing an uncertain fate, Loesch handed these documents over to the Americans in exchange for immunity for prosecution. Amongst them were dozens of items of correspondence between the Duke of Windsor and the Nazi high command, copies of which were then forwarded to Prime Minister Winston Churchill as a matter of the highest sensitivity. The PM subsequently discussed their contents with George VI and, just as *The Crown* shows, it was agreed that the papers should be sealed and suppressed.

In 1954, however, a small number of the papers were published, only to be followed by a much larger batch in July 1957. Within the Marburg papers were details of a Nazi plan to have the Duke of Windsor ally with their cause on the understanding that, in the event of a German victory, he and Wallis would assume the throne of Great Britain as king and queen. Whilst the duke didn't explicitly reject any expressions of interest by the Nazis, however, nor is there any evidence to suggest that he seriously considered accepting the terms. Because no conclusive evidence exists, debate over the extent to which he sympathised with Nazi ideology have raged for decades. The duke was certainly happy to engage in extensive discussions with Nazi Germany and believed that the UK should seek an alliance with Hitler. He subsequently opined that only aggressive bombing of Great Britain would bring the country to heel. Only later did the Duke of Windsor attempt to disavow all knowledge of what were proven to be close connections to senior Nazis. *The Crown* is right to say that the Duke and Duchess visited Nazi Germany; they made the trip in 1937 and were personally received by Adolf Hitler. To this day, it is not known exactly what Hitler and the duke discussed during their private audience.

As the Duke of Windsor arrives in the UK for the funeral of his friend, Edward "Fruity" Metcalfe, he little suspects that the Marburg papers are about to burst wide open. However, the duke actually came to England for Metcalfe's memorial several months after their publication, so would have been well aware of their existence by then. Equally confusing is the presence of Lady Alexandre Metcalfe, seen here as a grieving widow despite having been divorced from Fruity for years by the time of his death.

Likewise, whilst Billy Graham did preach at Windsor in 1955, the episode places him in the pulpit in November 1957, as the Duke of Windsor is mourning Fruity's death. Indeed, the private meeting between Graham and the queen that is shown in *Marionettes* appears to have been a bit of writerly indulgence. There is no record of such a meeting ever happening. In addition, whilst it's certainly satisfying to see Her Majesty sending her uncle away from England forever as a pariah after she learns of his enthusiasm for the Nazi cause, this didn't happen. A full ten years after the events depicted in *Marionettes*, the duke was invited to the unveiling of the Marlborough House memorial to Queen Mary. Regardless of the contents of the Marburg papers and the duke's personal politics, he was never fully excluded from the royal family by Queen Elizabeth II.

One last note: the photographs of the Duke and Duchess of Windsor socialising with senior Nazis that close the episode were not created for *The Crown*. They are unquestionably real.

2.7 Matrimonium

The Crown

Wounded by the news of Peter Townsend's forthcoming marriage to a much younger woman, Princess Margaret pressures Antony Armstrong-Jones to propose, little suspecting that he may already be expecting a baby with another woman. Whilst the queen has her suspicions, the princess is blissfully unaware of the secret the Palace is keeping from her as she prepares for her 1960 wedding.

The Truth

Peter Townsend – remember him? – is back, which means it's another Princess Margaret episode and one in which our flighty younger sister actually thinks that she might get her happy ending. Stay tuned on that one, dear readers.

You may remember that when Townsend and Margaret split, they pledged that if they couldn't marry each other, then they wouldn't marry at all. Though Margaret nearly broke their pact with her aborted engagement to Billy Wallace, it's Group Captain Townsend who finally puts a stake through it. Whilst stationed in Brussels, he fell in love with 19-year-old tobacco heiress Marie-Luce Jamagne. The couple eventually married in 1959 and remained together until Townsend's death; at the time of the wedding, the bride was 20 and the groom a quarter of a century her senior.

Margaret is understandably devastated at the conclusion of her doomed romance and her efforts to move on are the centrepiece of *Matrimonium*. Well, that and Tony Armstrong-Jones's apparent efforts to sleep with half of swinging London in one hour of television. Pearl clutchers beware, because *Matrimonium* is very heavy on sauce and we get to see Tony making out with some fictional old flames and some real ones too, including actress Jacqui Chan. As Tony makes a tour of the bedrooms of polite society, *The Crown* suggests that Michael Adeane and Tommy Lascelles were asked to investigate his movements by the queen, who was concerned that Armstrong-Jones may not an appropriate suitor for her sister. According to Morgan, they discovered that Camilla Fry was pregnant with the unsuspecting photographer's child. If *The Crown* is to be believed, the queen was so distressed to learn of this that she almost went into labour and was forced to take to her bed.

Thanks to the royal doctors and plenty of bedrest, disaster is averted and Elizabeth decides to keep the gossip to herself, unable to bring herself to ruin her sister's happy ever after. So Margaret finally gets her Westminster Abbey wedding on 6 May 1960, blissfully unaware that three weeks later his lover, Camilla, would give birth to their daughter, Polly. Incidentally, Armstrong-Jones's initial choice for best man was Camilla's husband, Jeremy Fry, but he was forced to step down after he was prosecuted for a homosexual liaison. *The Crown* actually drops Tony into bed with both of the Frys for a menage á trois but, as far as we know, that's just a bit of scriptwriter's fancy. *Matrimonium* is clear on one thing though: Tony knows nothing of his role in Polly's conception.

So, what *actually* happened between Tony and the Frys? He was indeed the father of Camilla Fry's daughter, Polly, and his paternity was proven by a DNA test more than four decades later. Although Armstrong-Jones, by then Lord Snowdon, denied having taken the test and Fry also denied his wife's claims that paternity had been proven, the game was up. Four years later, once Jeremy Fry was dead, Antony Armstrong-Jones admitted that he was indeed Polly's father.

This episode has a couple of very odd assertions in amongst the bare bottoms. First is that Armstrong-Jones was driven to propose to Margaret in order to win the approval of his mother, Anne, Countess of Rosse. Whilst he and the countess had a very rocky relationship, she knew a thing or two about social climbing herself, which the episode singularly fails to acknowledge. In addition, *Matrimonium* presents Margaret as a mercurial, wild-eyed gal who is obsessive about getting to the altar ahead of Townsend and his bride. In fact, Peter Townsend and Marie-Luce were married in December 1959, two months after their engagement was announced. Margaret later admitted that she had received a letter from Townsend informing her of his plans to marry in the morning post and accepted Tony's proposal that same evening. Confusingly, though, Margaret is already flashing her engagement sparkler when Tony catches the results of the 1959 general election, which was actually held four months before the princess's engagement was made public.

The show suggests that Margaret and Tony were secretly already engaged when Margaret surprised her sister with the announcement. In fact, Armstrong-Jones personally sought the queen's permission to propose to Margaret during a visit to Sandringham. *The Crown* then suggests that Margaret was forced to conceal her engagement for months so she wouldn't steal the limelight from the imminent arrival of Prince Andrew. In reality, Elizabeth was mere weeks away from delivering Andrew and asked if the official engagement announcement could be held back until she had given birth. It was a matter of weeks, not months, and simply an arrangement between sisters rather than an act of spite or some weird bit of royal protocol. Incidentally, Philip played squash as Prince Charles was born, rather than as his wife delivered Prince Andrew, as depicted in this episode.

One final note: during the scenes of the wedding ceremony, keep an eye peeled for footage of the real happy couple making their engagement announcement. And look fast for news footage of the real Princess Margaret travelling by carriage towards Westminster Abbey as sadly that's all we get to see of the longed-for wedding of our favourite (or perhaps not) flighty princess.

2.8 Dear Mrs Kennedy

The Crown

When the Kennedys bring Camelot to Buckingham Palace, the queen is stung to hear that Jackie made backhanded comments about her after the bash. Keen to prove her statesperson credentials, Elizabeth personally intervenes when Ghanian President Kwame Nkrumah expresses a wish to ally with the Soviet Union. In Dallas in 1963, tragedy strikes.

The Truth

Ah, the Kennedys. It was inevitable they were going to turn up, but their depiction is both slight and, let's be honest, disappointing. I've done a lot of tubthumping about the lack of female voices in *The Crown* but here's an episode that does give us a woman's perspective. Unfortunately, what we get is a bit of girl-against-girl jealousy and a big dollop of bitching. Given the rich opportunities offered by the meeting between Jackie Kennedy and Queen Elizabeth II, it's hugely disappointing.

Still.

The episode opens in 1960, as the newly elected President Kwame Nkrumah of Ghana espouses his wish to unite the African nations in pursuit of their own interests, rather than those of the Commonwealth. As we watch Elizabeth's portrait being removed and replaced with one of Lenin, we have our set up for *Dear Mrs Kennedy*: will Ghana distance itself from the West in favour of pursuing deeper connections with the Soviet Union?

The Kennedys really did pay a visit to Buckingham Palace to meet the queen on 5 June 1961 and in fact, though the show doesn't depict it, Princess Alice, Philip's mother, also attended. That feels like a lost opportunity, though wouldn't have fit in with the later narrative of Philip not having seen his mother for an age. Likewise, whether the queen really did spend hours earnestly gazing at Norman Hartnell gowns in an effort to outdo the glamourous Jackie Kennedy is one that I'll leave up to you. Equally questionable is the production's assertion that the Kennedys got both the queen and Duke of Edinburgh's titles wrong during their official reception. Quite apart from the fact that they would have been well-drilled in the correct protocol and forms of address, Joseph Kennedy,

JFK's father, was an American ambassador at the Court of St James's and Kennedy had spent time living in London: they were not hayseeds. Yet *The Crown* slaps on the uncouth Americans angle with a trowel. And not for the last time.

The queen tours Jackie around the palace and believes that she has made a friend. Afterwards she is disappointed and hurt to learn from Princess Margaret that Mrs Kennedy actually made disparaging remarks about the royal family, the queen and the dinner at a party. In fact, she specifically picked on the queen's age and lack of intellectual capacity, two things guaranteed to get the royal goat.

That would be a bombshell, right? Well yes, if it were true; whilst Mrs Kennedy did regale her friends with gossip about the event, if Cecil Beaton and Gore Vidal were to be believed, she wasn't quite so vicious as *Dear Mrs Kennedy* suggests. Jackie was unimpressed by Buckingham Palace itself and found little to admire in the queen's frock and hairdo. It wasn't exactly gracious, but nor is there any evidence that the queen heard about it, especially via Princess Margaret. Vidal, however, unsurprisingly made sure that Margaret knew full well that Mrs Kennedy had found her sister heavy going; in reply, Margaret supposedly told him "that's what she's there for". It's really disappointing that this is the tack the show takes in order to give Her Majesty an excuse to do a bit of diplomatic dancing of her own. After all, what other motive could she have then wishing to outshine a younger and glitzier rival?

Desperate to prove her relevance, says *Dear Mrs Kennedy*, the sovereign went to Ghana and charmed Nkrumah into sticking with the Commonwealth, dancing the foxtrot with him until he was no longer able to resist her charms. Ironically, when Kennedy sees this, he congratulates Jackie on having made such an impact on foreign policy, suggesting that the queen went to Ghana only in order to win a catfight of international proportions.

It's nonsense, of course. The queen had actually been due to visit Ghana as part of a wider tour in 1959, but the trip had to be postponed because of her pregnancy. Whilst the tour, which was rescheduled for November 1961, was controversial, it certainly wasn't arranged almost overnight as *The Crown* suggests. The episode also does the Ghanian reception dirty, reducing as it does an exceptionally grand ceremony to an awkward and badly organised photo opportunity in *Dear Mrs Kennedy*.

Though the foxtrot between the queen and the president made headlines, it wasn't motivated by Elizabeth's desire to get one over on Mrs Kennedy. Nor did Her Majesty singlehandedly convince Nkrumah to reverse his approach to the Soviets, a policy that Ghana pursued even after that infamous foxtrot. In reality, the British government felt that the situation in Ghana was too volatile to guarantee the queen's safety, but she insisted on going. To reduce this to a matter of female one upmanship does her a disservice and misses the chance to mine the queen's growth into a monarch who knows her own mind against the men in grey suits. And of course, *The Crown* can't resist showing us Macmillan's shock when news of the fabulous foxtrot reaches him. In reality, he knew full well what an impact it would make on the Americans, whom he was keen to involve in the Ghanaian issue. What Macmillan particularly wanted was American money to put into the Volta Dam project; without it, Ghana might well have turned to the Soviets for the required funding. "I have risked my queen," Macmillan supposedly told Kennedy later. "You must risk your money."

The depiction of the Kennedys is far from flattering. Not only are they portrayed as clueless in matters of protocol, but *The Crown* can't help but hint at violence, philandering and narcotics, no doubt prescribed by Kennedy's favourite physician, Dr "Feelgood" Jacobson, aka "Miracle Max", who eventually lost his license. It's a whole lot to pack into one episode, but *Dear Mrs Kennedy* isn't done yet. Mortified by the realisation that the queen must have heard about her backbiting, Jackie makes a totally fictional trip to Windsor to apologise to Elizabeth for her misplaced comments. Whilst Jackie did return to the UK before travelling home to the United States, it wasn't to see the queen. All in all, this episode makes for a pretty OTT outing.

And because it's the Kennedys, the show can't resist flashing forward to the moment when the queen learns that JFK has been assassinated in Dallas. Elizabeth's request that the court go into mourning and the bell at Westminster Abbey be rung for the late president against the usual protocol, which reserves these gestures for royals, is accurate. Curiously, whilst she was pregnant with Prince Edward, there's no sign of that pregnancy in these scenes.

Finally, it would be lovely to see the Queen Mother do something other than eat and complain. She had a full court calendar throughout the era, yet *The Crown* shows her doing very little beyond watching TV and munching carbs. Such is royal life.

2.9 Paterfamilias

The Crown

Against his wife's wishes, Philip sends Prince Charles to his old school, the unforgiving Scottish institution of Gordonstoun. During their journey north, the duke recalls the tragic loss of his beloved sister, whilst young Charles prepares for the ordeal that awaits him.

The Truth

After an episode dedicated to women trying to outdo women, we're back in *The Crown*'s favoured territory of male stories for *Paterfamilias*, in which Elizabeth and Philip clash over the education of Prince Charles. The queen is keen for her sensitive son to go to Eton and, though she has little to say on the matter in this episode, in reality the Queen Mother advocated for Eton too. Philip, meanwhile, was determined that the heir to the throne should attend Gordonstoun, the Scottish school where he himself was educated. Charles and dapper uncle Dickie Mountbatten are delighted at the prospect of Eton, even heading to Savile Row to get kitted out, before the Duke of Edinburgh spoils everybody's fun and demands that Charles head north.

And that's where we flashback to a mostly fictional storyline that seems determined to give Philip some motivation for his general surliness and the chip he has on his shoulder.

Paterfamilias takes us all the way back to Germany in 1934, where we see Philip trying on his own school uniform. As he does, he's accompanied by his Swastika-wearing brother-in-law, George Donatus of Greece, aka Don. Philip's sister, Princess Cecilie (known as Cécile) and her husband were indeed Nazi supporters, even if they weren't yet members of the party. Though the armband he wears succeeds in driving the point home, Don wasn't a card-carrying member of the National Socialists until 1937.

The Crown has already drip-fed us plenty of information about Philip's distant relationship with his parents and, in this episode, it creates the fiction that he was virtually raised by Cécile and her husband, but that really wasn't the truth. Though he did spend a lot of time with the couple, Philip had routinely been shunted from relative to relative –

including his grandmother, Queen Victoria, and between homes and schools. Much of this instability could be attributed to the absence of his father, Prince Andrew of Greece and Denmark, who preferred the high life in Monte Carlo, whilst the parlous mental health of Philip's mother confined her to a sanatorium for much of her son's childhood.

During his years in Germany, Philip was a student at Schule Schloss Salem, which was founded by Jewish educationalist Kurt Hahn. Hahn's outspoken opposition to the rise of Naziism had resulted in brief imprisonment in 1933, following his heartfelt plea to the students and faculty of Salem to choose between the school or Hitler. When he was released following an appeal by British prime minister Ramsay MacDonald, Hahn fled the country and settled in Scotland, where he established the hard-line school, Gordonstoun. It was here that the young prince was to complete his education. Despite the depiction of Philip's journey to Gordonstoun with Cécile in *The Crown*, however, he was actually accompanied by another sister, Theodora. As the young and nervous Philip travels to the school, Cécile regales him with the tale of Hahn's past, from his career in Germany to his flight to safety and the founding of Gordonstoun. It's presented as though all of this is news to Philip, despite the fact that he would've been very well aware of who the headmaster was, since he'd already studied at an institution founded by Kurt Hahn.

In the parallel stories, both Charles and Philip suffer miserably through the strict school regime. Charles did have an unhappy time at Gordonstoun, where he struggled with the highly physical nature of a curriculum which was at odds with his more artistic sensibilities. It was during these unhappy years that he bonded with Mountbatten, just as he'd been a champion to Philip earlier. Dickie was to become a grandfather figure to Charles for the rest of his life. But it's in the depiction of Philip's years that *Paterfamilias* really falls into the realm of fiction.

As Philip begs the pregnant Cécile to let him come home to Germany, she tells him that she will gladly host him for half term and thus turn down an invitation she has received to a family wedding in London. Though he now has something to look forward to, Philip finds himself more miserable than ever; tormented by bullies and pushed to his limits, he eventually snaps and punches the ringleader in the face. Brought before Hahn, depicted here as a rather dull headmaster in contrast to the colourful and eccentric figure he truly was, Philip learns that he is to be punished. He will be kept back at Gordonstoun during half term, where he will singlehandedly build a wall, rather than head to Germany and his sister's supportive shoulder. As a result, a disappointed Cécile decides to attend the wedding instead. As you might have guessed, tragedy ensues and she is killed in a plane crash en route to England.

Except none of this happened and Philip certainly wasn't subsequently tormented by his role in his favourite sister's death, because he had no such role. There was never any plan for Philip to go to Germany and stay with Cécile, who always planned to travel to England for the wedding of Don's brother, Ludwig. Fearful of air travel, the heavily pregnant Cécile went into labour during the fateful fog-bound flight and the plane crashed into a factory chimney near Ostend as it attempted to land, killing everyone on board. Among the victims were Cécile, Don, their two sons and Cécile's newborn baby boy. That the accident on 16 November 1937 was a tragedy that broke Philip's heart is beyond question. That it was in any way attributable to a change of plans forced by his bad behaviour is utterly make believe.

In order to compound Philip's sense of isolation, the episode adds a scene in which he attends the family funerals in Germany. Despite Mountbatten's supportive presence, the young prince cuts a tragic figure and his grief is only made all the more acute by his mother's failure to recognise him at the funeral. The message is clear: he is totally alone in the world but for Mountbatten.

But he wasn't.

Princess Alice's heath was recovering at the time of the tragedy and though devastated by the death of her daughter and grandchildren, she had taken the news with stoicism. Philip and his mother had been in recent contact and were making plans to see one another, yet *The Crown* turns her into a barely-functioning zombie. In a final insult to the historical record, Philip's brother, Prince Andrew, remonstrates with young Philip in front of the mourners, blaming him for their sister's death. It's nonsense; Andrew was devastated by the tragedy, but he certainly didn't blame Philip for it.

As history shows, Philip didn't return to Gordonstoun immediately after the funeral. Instead, he spent Christmas in the UK before joining members of his family in Italy, yet *The Crown* packs him off to Gordonstoun to single-handedly build a fictional wall and learn an important lesson about family, friends, and the greater community. By the time the wall is finished, Philip has found his place: Gordonstoun will turn him into the athletic, go-getting and, let's be honest, surly character *The Crown* so adores.

Back in the present, however, Charles is anything but settling in. Instead, he is dependent on his detective, Donald Green, who really was a close confidante to the young prince, and is berated by his furious father on the trip home from Scotland. As Charles sobs, Philip pilots their light aircraft with an astonishing lack of care for someone who supposedly blames himself for the death of his sister in a plane crash. So distressed is the young prince that, as soon as they arrive back at Windsor, Charles dashes off into the arms of his waiting nanny as the queen watches from a distance. And so, the foundations are laid on thick for season three.

One thing before we move on: it's perhaps telling that both of Charles's own children were schooled at Eton.

2.10 Mystery Man

The Crown

As the Profumo affair rocks British society, speculation grows over the identity of a mystery man seen in a photograph taken at a party thrown by Stephen Ward, the osteopath who has been treating Philip for a neck injury.

The last thing the Palace wants is for the Duke of Edinburgh to be sucked into the sordid case of Christine Keeler and John Profumo. But will they have any choice?

The Truth

And so to the closing episode of season two and the last bow of (most of) our initial cast. As the 1960s draw on, who can blame *The Crown* for capping its tale of royal marital discord with a dip into the epoch-defining Profumo affair? *Mystery Man* sets up the intriguing premise that Prince Philip, after seeking treatment for a cricked neck from osteopath Stephen Ward, may have attended Ward's infamous parties, where powerful establishment figures mingled with sex workers and brought down a government. Perhaps fearful of ruffling legal feathers, though, whilst the series doesn't confirm that the Duke of Edinburgh dabbled, an on-screen drawing of a man seen at the parties is unmistakeably Philip.

The Profumo affair could only have happened in the 1960s. In a nutshell, Secretary of State for War John Profumo was conducting an affair with Ward's friend Christine Keeler at the same time as she was conducting an affair with Yevgeny Ivanov, Soviet naval attaché to the Russian embassy in London. He was also, more worryingly, a Soviet spy. With the world embroiled in a seething Cold War, two such opposing political figures sharing pillow talk with the same woman was a recipe for disaster. When the press identified Profumo as the mystery man in a photograph taken at one of scandalous Ward's parties, the story gripped the nation. It would become a defining incident of the 1960s.

The Profumo scandal was a national fascination to such an extent that, when Stephen Ward took his own life during the trial, his lifeless body was photographed by press vultures seeking a story. Indeed, the Ward/Keeler scenes are pretty much on the money. What's surprising for a programme that loves a bit of scandal is how little of it is shown. We glimpse the main players, but they're scarcely even supporting characters.

Just as *Mystery Man* shows, Macmillan supported Profumo's claims that he was the victim of false allegations. By throwing his weight behind the erring minister, when the truth came out, Macmillan was shown up as a man of faulty judgment who could scarcely control his government. Seen as the relic of an establishment that was crumbling, both the electorate and Macmillan's own party had had quite enough of his government.

The ailing PM wrote to the queen in 1963 and offered an apology, but made no allusions to resignation; in the end, he resigned following an operation on his prostate on 10 October. Whilst the operation was a success and Macmillan could have returned to the role that he had longed for, just like Anthony Eden before him, he knew that his time had come. Eden's ill health had given him a reason to resign before he was pushed or voted out, saving a little face at least; now so-called Supermac's prostate operation had gifted him the same excuse. He handed in his resignation a little over a week after he had undergone surgery, believing to the end that he had been the victim of a plot to oust him.

The Crown takes a rather more dramatic tack in the matter of the prime minister's fate, as viewers see the queen initially refusing to accept Macmillan's resignation due to her preoccupation with her pregnancy. She eventually capitulates when the PM's health takes a turn for the worse. This didn't happen, but it places the queen in the centre of events in a way that will become increasingly unusual as we move through the seasons.

Oddly, just as the show ignored the political skulduggery which saw Macmillan appointed against Eden's wishes and now breezes over the shenanigans which secured the succession of Macmillan's favourite, Alec Douglas-Home, over perennial bridesmaid Rab Butler. With Butler regarded by many as his natural successor, Macmillan moved fast to advise the queen to appoint Douglas-Home before the wider Conservative Party could reach a consensus. Realising that Douglas-Home might not be able to overcome opposition from the supporters of other candidates for the role, the queen invited the politician to see if he could form a government. Twenty-four hours later, he was able to confirm that he could; Alec Douglas-Home was appointed prime minister before members of the wider Conservative Party had a chance to have any say in the matter. Supermac had managed to get his own man into the role, regardless of what his opponents had wanted.

So, was Prince Philip the mystery man of the title? The press seemed to think so and there were suspicions that Prince Philip might have been one of Ward's clients in more than an osteopathic sense. These claims initially surfaced in 1963, but with no concrete evidence to back them up, they went no further than tabloid hints. However, Ward was a keen artist who often sketched members of the establishment, including Prince Philip, so being drawn by Stephen Ward was certainly no indication that a person was involved in more saucy matters. In fact, Ward's sketches of Philip, Margaret and other members of the royal family were made during arranged sittings at Buckingham Palace to answer a commission from the *Illustrated London News*. Hardly a secret shame.

And so we finally confront the fictional affair with ballet dancer Ulanova, which initially reared its head in episode one of the season. Confronted by Elizabeth, Philip swerves an outright denial, but pledges his love and loyalty to her. And that's that. After hours and hours of marital discord, the couple are once again united as they look forward to the birth of their fourth and last child. Margaret and Tony are also expecting a second happy event, though they're more concerned with renovating their Kensington Palace apartments, much to the annoyance of their royal neighbours.

There's a moment that no doubt made fans of all things swinging smile, as *Mystery Man* treats fans of satire to a recreation of the sixties legendary *Beyond the Fringe*, the show that made stars out of Peter Cook, Dudley Moore, Alan Bennett and Jonathan Miller. Kudos to Macmillan for managing to see the show in London in 1963, because it was actually being performed on Broadway by then. Never mind. In reality, Supermac attended a performance in 1962 and was indeed spotted in the audience by an eagle-eyed and waspishly-minded Peter Cook. As *Mystery Man* accurately depicts, he tried and failed to hide behind his programme. Incidentally, the queen went along to see *Beyond the Fringe* too. And she particularly enjoyed the way it skewered Macmillan.

One last thing to note regarding this episode is a curious coincidence of timing. Christine Keeler retreated from the public eye once her notoriety faded and lived a private life away from the cameras. Long out of the limelight, she died just a few days after the premiere of *The Crown*'s second season.

The series ends on a family photograph, with the newborn Prince Edward taking centre stage. And for our season one and two cast, that's that. We've been through war, abdication, sex and scandal, but we've barely even started.

Right: When *The Crown* hit Netflix, it took the world by storm, just like the romance of the young Elizabeth and Philip decades earlier. (Fotocollectie Anefo, public domain)

Below: *The Crown* tells the story of Queen Elizabeth II's tumultuous reign, beyond the happy ever afters. (Fotocollectie Anefo, public domain)

The Crown's Queen Mary is a bastion of imperious seen-it-all sangfroid. That's not a million miles away from the real thing! (Wellcome Collection, public domain)

Queen Elizabeth II's father never wanted to be king, but he stepped up to do his duty to the crown. (Library of Congress Prints and Photographs Division, public domain)

Above: The Queen Mother really did blame the abdication of her brother-in-law, the Duke of Windsor, for the early death of her husband, King George VI. (Fotocollectie Anefo, public domain)

Right: Whatever the series might want us to think, Queen Mary wasn't to blame for the murder of the Romanov family. (Public domain)

Above: The Duke and Duchess of Windsor, aka Edward and Mrs Simpson, are arguably given a rather sympathetic portrayal by *The Crown*. (Daily Herald Archive at the National Media Museum)

Left: Princess Alice of Battenberg is all nun, all the time in *The Crown*. The reality was a little different. (Public domain)

Winston Churchill is a central figure in the series, though his relationship with the Queen was rather more friendly than that we see on screen. (Library of Congress, public domain)

In life as on screen, Lord Mountbatten was a father figure to Prince Philip and a grandfather figure to Prince Charles. His murder shocked the nation. (Fotocollectie Anefo, public domain)

Left: When *The Crown* pointed the finger at the Duke of Edinburgh for the death of his sister, Princess Cecilie, some viewers felt as though fiction had gone too far. (Public domain)

Below: Winston Churchill and Anthony Eden were friends and rivals, much to the joy of *The Crown*'s scriptwriters. (Fotocollectie Anefo, public domain)

Seen here with the royal family as they celebrate the christening of Prince Charles, the Queen Mother wasn't quite the telly and carb-addict the series suggests. (Fotocollectie Anefo, public domain)

Whilst *The Crown* is at pains to drive home their cold parenting style, the Queen and Prince Philip, seen here with Prince Charles, Princess Anne and the family dogs, tried to balance parenthood and service. (Wellcome Collection, public domain)

Left: Group Captain Peter Townsend, a hero of the Battle of Britain, captured the public imagination when he romanced a besotted Princess Margaret. (Mr BJ Daventry, Royal Air Force Official Photographer, public domain)

Below: Whatever the series might say, Prince Philip wasn't really obsessed with the Apollo 11 landings and the three astronauts on the crew were anything but wide-eyed hicks. (NASA, public domain)

Above: Though society darlings Princess Margaret and her husband, Antony Armstrong-Jones, Lord Snowdon, commanded crowds wherever they went, their marriage wasn't a happy one. (Fotocollectie Anefo, public domain)

Right: Harold Wilson was rumoured to be one of the Queen's favourite prime ministers; his early departure plunged the House of Commons into turmoil. (Allan Warren, CC BY SA 3.0)

Above: When is the Royal Yacht Britannia not the Royal Yacht Britannia? When it's a metaphor for the crumbling monarchy in *The Crown*. (Ben Salter/Oxyman/ Wikimedia Commons, CC BY 2.0)

Left: *The Crown* suggests that Princess Diana's nerves failed her when she climbed Uluru. In fact, it was the Princess of Wales's skirt that wasn't up to the climb. (John Hill, CC BY-SA 4.0)

A divisive figure even now, Margaret Thatcher always made sure to leave her wellies at home whenever a visit to Balmoral loomed. (Margaret Thatcher Foundation, copyrighted free use)

As his mother's protector, viewers have seen Prince William grow from a babe in Princess Diana's arms into a young man in love. (John MacIntyre/ Paisley Scotland, CC BY 2.0)

Left: Tony Blair swept into government on a landslide, but his request to the Queen to "call me Tony" fell on deaf ears. (HM Government, OGL 3)

Below: Though her life both before and after her marriage to Timothy Laurence was anything but dull, *The Crown* has given Princess Anne oddly short shrift, ignoring everything from sporting triumphs to attempted kidnapping. (The United States Amy Band, CC BY 2.0)

Above: The depiction of the death and funeral of Diana, Princess of Wales, and Dodi Fayed – not to mention its aftermath – proved controversial for Netflix. (Bobak Ha'Eri/Wikimedia Commons, CC BY 2.5)

Right: Thanks to his well-publicised relationship with Netflix, viewers and press alike waited to see what kind of a ride Prince Harry would be given by Peter Morgan. (Eva Rinaldi/Wikimedia Commons, CC BY SA 2.0)

Mohamed Al-Fayed's early years proved fertile ground for *The Crown*'s scriptwriters, especially his supposed – actually fictional - obsession with the Duke and Duchess of Windsor. (Abi Skipp/Wikimedia Commons, CC BY 2.0)

Martin Bashir's infamous *Panorama* interview with Princess Diana was a major part of *The Crown*, much to the chagrin of some viewers. (Luigi Novi/Nightscream/Wikimedia Commons, CC BY 3.0)

The Crown didn't quite get as far as the wedding of Prince Harry and Meghan Markle... but never say never. (Northern Ireland Office, CC BY 2.0)

Left: Though viewers were held rapt by the romantic comings and goings of Prince Charles and Camilla Parker Bowles, history tells that it worked out okay in the end for King Charles III and Queen Camilla. (Isaac Mayne/DCMS, PDM-Owner)

Below: *The Crown* has taken viewers through more than half a century of the monarchy, introducing us to generations of royals. (Magnus D/Wikimedia Commons, CC BY 2.0)

Seasons 3 and 4

Notable Cast

Queen Elizabeth II	Olivia Colman
Prince Philip, Duke of Edinburgh	Tobias Menzies
Margaret Thatcher	Gillian Anderson
Queen Elizabeth The Queen Mother	Marion Bailey
Princess Margaret	Helena Bonham Carter
Denis Thatcher	Stephen Boxer
Michael Fagan	Tom Brooke
Wallis, Duchess of Windsor	Geraldine Chaplin
Lady Diana Spencer	Emma Corrin
Louis, 1st Earl Mountbatten of Burma	Charles Dance
Antony Armstrong-Jones, 1st Earl of Snowdon	Ben Daniels
Anne, Princess Royal	Erin Doherty
Michael Shea	Nicholas Farrell
Camilla Shand	Emerald Fennell
Prince Edward, Duke of Windsor	Derek Jacobi
Princess Alice	Jane Lapotaire
Sir Winston Churchill	John Lithgow
Charles, Prince of Wales	Josh O'Connor
Bob Hawke	Richard Roxburghe
Harold Wilson	Jason Watkins
Sir Anthony Blunt	Samuel West

℥⟨ SEASON 3 ⟩℥

3.1 Olding

The Crown

As the nation welcomes Labour's Harold Wilson as prime minister, the disbelieving queen is shocked to learn from an ailing Winston Churchill that Wilson enjoys ties to the KGB. However, when she sees the new premier conversing with shadowy figures at Churchill's funeral, she begins to wonder if there's more to it than just conjecture.

With palace gossip swirling around Wilson's Soviet connections and Princess Margaret's crumbling marriage to Lord Snowdon, Her Majesty is stunned to learn that the true Soviet mole may be a little closer to home. In fact, the Surveyor of the Queen's Pictures, Sir Anthony Blunt, has been hiding in plain sight as a pillar of the establishment and KGB double agent for decades.

The Truth

Season three of *The Crown* brings with it a fresh cast and launches us into 1964, the same year in which season two ended. But this is a new era and to drive the point home, the queen is attending the presentation of a new stamp, in which her Dorothy Wilding photographic portrait will be replaced by Arnold Machin's newer design. In reality, this switch didn't happen until 1967. Likewise, the stroke which Churchill suffers in the opening scenes of the episode actually took place in January 1965.

But stamps aren't what we're here for, because *Olding* is all about secrets and spies.

As Harold Wilson sweeps into Downing Street at the head of the new Labour government. Prince Philip senses revolution in the air and Her Majesty enjoys a stilted meeting with the timid Wilson, who is star struck in the monarch's presence. In fact, he'd actually known her for two decades. In addition, it's a shame that *Olding* depicts the anxious PM nervously awaiting his audience with Her Majesty alone, since he actually arrived at the palace with his wife and family in tow.

And what a start for him it is. No sooner has Wilson squirmed and stuttered his way through the audience than he's the centre of palace gossip. In fact, the queen is surprised by rumours at a private dinner that Wilson is actually a mole for the KGB.

There's a lot of timeline oddness in this episode, as the family learn that Churchill has died whilst the Duke of Gloucester is celebrating his birthday. Yet the duke's birthday fell in late March and Churchill passed away in late January. As we know by now though, *The Crown* has always existed in its very own timeline.

What is true, however, is that there were rumours linking Wilson to the KGB, just as this episode purports. Whilst MI5 kept a file on the PM though, the rumours were eventually proved to be unfounded: the security services concluded after decades of surveillance that the prime minister had no relationship with the KGB, either official or otherwise. Equally true is that Sir Anthony Blunt, the Surveyor of the Queen's Pictures, was one of the notorious Cambridge Five.

The Cambridge Five was the collective name given to Blunt along with Donald Maclean, Guy Burgess, Kim Philby and John Cairncross. The five men were recruited by the Soviet security services whilst studying at the University of Cambridge; the incredibly well-connected Blunt was the man who sniffed out likely candidates and recruited them to the cause. Each of the five men went on to enjoy a high flying role in the British government, but despite being accepted at the very heart of the establishment, their loyalty was to Russia. For decades, they served as double agents without arousing so much as a hint of suspicion.

Blunt was recruited by the Soviet Union in the 1930s and acted as a double agent whilst in the employment of MI5, passing information back to his KGB spymasters. He confessed to his involvement in the passing of British secrets to the Soviets on 23 April 1964, having received guaranteed immunity from prosecution and a promise to seal his confession for 15 years. Blunt's blackmail of Prince Philip over his involvement with the sordid Profumo affair is a fictional touch, but his continued employment isn't. Having been appointed as the Surveyor of the King's Pictures in 1945, he remained in his royal role after the succession of Elizabeth II and retained the position for nearly thirty years. In 1956, this apparent bastion of the establishment was knighted.

Blunt's confession was sealed as an official secret and he continued in his illustrious role at the palace until his retirement in 1972. Believing that making his confession public would show up Britain's security services as inept, Blunt wrongly assumed that nobody would ever know what he had done. However, the guarantee that his confession would remain secret was only good for fifteen years and when the time was up, he discovered that he had been naïve to think that the government would continue to keep the matter to themselves.

Blunt's carefully constructed cover fell apart in 1979 when he was exposed as a Soviet mole by Margaret Thatcher in the House of Commons. He was hounded by the press and stripped of his knighthood and honours; retreating from the public eye to concentrate on his art history interests, Anthony Blunt died in 1983.

3.2 Margaretology

The Crown

Princess Margaret and Lord Snowdon are making a splash in the USA, where Margaret is the toast of every town even as the disappointed Snowdon seems to be little more than her support act. Yet Margaret's charms may be just what the country needs to secure some much needed money from America, where President Johnson is refusing to support British requests for a bailout in retaliation for the UK's lack of support during the Vietnam War.

Whilst Margaret charms the president and secures the cash, Prince Philip warns his wife that her sister can't be trusted with more responsibility.

The Truth

In case we missed the sibling rivalry, this episode opens with a flashback to 1943, where a young Princess Elizabeth bemoans the fact that she will one day be queen. Little Princess Margaret, meanwhile, would saw off her right arm to rule and hastens to tell Tommy Lascelles that she wants the job. Needless to say, Tommy soon puts her straight and, it seems, lights the touchpaper on a lifelong resentment between the sisters.

The last we saw of Margaret in season two, she was happily marrying Antony Armstrong-Jones, now Lord Snowdon. But this is *The Crown* and, just as in real life, that happy ever after didn't last. In episode one of this season, she was drinking heavily and bemoaning her lot and things are no better in episode two, as the Earl and Countess of Snowdon travel to the USA for the launch of his new book. Of course, he's soon the supporting player: every eye is on Princess Margaret, as she gloatingly likes to remind him.

In fact, Tony wasn't even married to Margaret when he made his promotional book tour in 1958. He did, however, join her on an official visit to the US on behalf of the British government in 1965, which *The Crown* depicts. Well, to a point. It doesn't show many of the princess's official engagements, but we do get to see Margaret living her best life, partying and raising hell as the queen is stuck at home with Prince Philip's vests.

If you saw any marketing for this series you almost certainly saw a shot of Princess Margaret reclining decadently in a bubble bath wearing the Poltimore Tiara, which she had also worn at her wedding. It's a recreation of a very famous photograph taken by Snowdon, but it wasn't taken in the United States. Though she took the tiara along with her on the tour, the photograph was snapped in Kensington Palace three years earlier and was one of those that provided inspiration for the events in *Beryl*.

Margaretology also departs from reality when Margaret is asked to attend a White House dinner as a last-minute favour to the government, since LBJ has refused to visit the UK and meet the queen. With the pound devalued and the country in desperate need of an American financial bailout, someone needs to charm the socks off President Johnson. He is deliberately dodging the Windsors in a fit of pique at Britain's refusal to support American efforts in Vietnam, says the script, even suggesting that Johnson went so far as to avoid Churchill's funeral. It's juicy, but it's not accurate: LBJ was actually unable to travel due to illness. Despite it being doctor's orders that Johnson remain on bedrest whilst recovering from influenza, the president faced condemnation for his decision to send his Vice President in his stead.

Whilst Johnson really was frustrated at Wilson's refusal to step up and offer support for the Vietnam War, he certainly didn't turn it into an international incident in 1965. Though *The Crown* depicts the boorish American deliberately snubbing a royal invitation to England, that invitation was never actually issued. No official royal invitation was issued to JFK either; contrary to the script, the queen only dined with the Kennedys as depicted in *Dear Mrs Kennedy* because they were visiting London on other business. Their visit was a banquet, not an official State Dinner.

When Elizabeth asks her to go to the White House, Margaret refuses to jump to it, using the excuse that she has to be in Manhattan to launch her husband's book. In reality, that launch took place in 1958 and she wasn't there. Left with no other choice in the face of her sibling's refusal, the queen decides to pull rank. She commands her little sister to go to Washington DC and charm the president, and she won't take no for an answer.

Of course, the dinner at the White House was anything but last minute: it had been on Margaret's itinerary for weeks, just as you might expect for a princess carrying out an official government visit on behalf of her country. Though *The Crown* doesn't ever like to acknowledge it, Princess Margaret wasn't just a boozy gadabout with a chip on her shoulder, but a working royal who was no stranger to undertaking diplomatic missions overseas. In fact, though the series suggests that she had never met President Johnson before, they had actually been introduced in 1962 during extravagant celebrations of Jamaica's independence. That's not half as dramatic though.

Naturally, when Margaret hits the White House she takes it by storm. She tells filthy jokes, dances up a riot with LBJ and even throws some serious shade at the late JFK. That she shone is a fact, but the filthy jokes are a matter of conjecture; likewise, given that LBJ had recently undergone surgery, it's unlikely that he got as royally drunk as *The Crown* suggests. There certainly wouldn't have been any spiteful comments about the late Jack Kennedy, since his mother was present at the same dinner and had taken tea with Margaret earlier on her tour. The main crux of this episode, namely that Margaret singlehandedly secured an American financial bailout for Britain, is totally fictional. Johnson had already agreed to support measures to delay the devaluation of the pound. It's also a falsehood to claim that the tour of America was a resounding success, as Americans were rather dubious of the princess's penchant for partying, boozing and treating people badly. They certainly didn't fawn over her as *The Crown* depicts.

When Margaret gets home and demands more responsibility, the queen bizarrely offers her the Order of Merit, the highest honour in her power to bestow and one that wouldn't be earned by a trip to the White House. Needless to say, this is another bit of make believe. In depicting Margaret as held back by sibling jealousy and refused responsibility because of her fabulous personality, *The Crown* resolutely fails to acknowledge that she already had an official and very active role as a senior royal. To present the queen as jealously refusing her an official role is total fiction. But *The Crown* will be beating the sisters at war drum for a little while yet, so we'd better get used to it.

3.3 Aberfan

The Crown

In 1966, tragedy strikes the little Welsh mining community of Aberfan when the pit tip collapses onto the village school, killing dozens of children and their teachers. Despite Wilson's attempts to convince the queen to visit, she refuses to go.

When the public turn on Elizabeth for her lack of compassion, Wilson confesses that the accusations started within his own cabinet. The queen backs down and visits Aberfan, though she admits that she had to fake her tears. Alone that evening, however, her grief is very real indeed.

The Truth

The Aberfan disaster is one of the defining moments of modern British history. On 21 October 1966, a pit tip above the village of Aberfan collapsed and caused a landslide that buried Pantglas Junior School, killing 116 children and 28 adults. The tragedy plunged the nation into mourning and left the community united in grief.

In *Aberfan*, the only person who doesn't seem to share that grief is the queen. Whilst Snowdon and Wilson travel to the village – in Snowdon's case to help with the rescue and recovery efforts – Her Majesty refuses to budge. She will not go to the scene, she says, because she would be a distraction rather than a help. Eventually, public criticism of her absence prompts Elizabeth to make the trip. Warned that she should give a public display of emotion, the queen manufactures some fake tears just to please the cameras. In reality, the scene in which she dabs at her dry eyes for the media did not happen, yet it is one of the most scathing depictions of Her Majesty shown in *The Crown*.

Aberfan really does make some strange decisions. Firstly, whilst Snowdon and Philip are shown as heroes of the hour, Snowdon digging through rubble and Philip sombrely representing the crown before angrily remonstrating with his wife about her indifference, this isn't quite as things were. Prompted by his Welsh heritage, Snowdon visited bereaved families rather than got hands on at the site of the landslide, whilst Philip, at the request of the queen, arrived the day after the disaster. The series has him wait a week before he is finally and reluctantly prised away from a duck shoot to make the trip: it's a fairly rotten portrayal of the couple all round. *The Crown* suggests that, fearing the government would be dragged into the hunt for someone to blame, Wilson's camp deliberately deflected public and press attention onto the queen's apparent inaction in order to smokescreen their own failings, but that conceals the reality. Plans were already being made for the queen and Prince Philip to visit Aberfan: their decision to do so certainly wasn't a panicked reaction to bad press.

Things get even odder when Elizabeth confides in Wilson that there is something wrong with her: an inability to show emotion in public. In fact, the initial explanation the queen offers for her reluctance to visit Aberfan is identical to that offered in reality: Her Majesty was mindful that her presence would merely slow the rescue efforts and provide an unwelcome distraction. That was why the queen's visit was planned for the time when the desperate rescue efforts were concluding. In addition, those who were with the queen when she visited Aberfan on 29 October commented later on how truly upset she was: to suggest that she dabbed at dry eyes just to please the press is unnecessarily savage. Equally, *The Crown* shows Elizabeth alone in Aberfan, but Philip accompanied her on the trip, as well as on a return visit more than thirty years later.

After piling on the critiques, the episode ends with the solitary queen wiping away a tear as she listens to the hymn sung at the funeral of those who lost their lives in Aberfan. It is a more sympathetic depiction than the rest of *Aberfan* allows. And it honestly feels like a shame.

3.4 Bubbikins

The Crown

When Prince Philip's mother, Princess Alice of Battenberg, comes under threat from the imposition of military rule in Athens, Elizabeth invites her to live at Buckingham Palace, against Philip's wishes. As she settles in, the royal family embark on an ill-fated documentary that is intended to prove they are no different to normal people, only to have it backfire.

To everyone's surprise, Princess Alice saves the day by giving a charming and candid interview to *The Guardian*, which salvages not only the reputation of the House of Windsor, but her relationship with her son, Philip.

The Truth

If Aberfan was a queasy mix of truth and fiction, then *Bubbikins* is a lot lighter on the facts and a lot heavier on the make believe. As Athens is seized by a military junta in 1967, we see Princess Alice, aka the mother of the Duke of Edinburgh, pacing within the walls of her order, the Christian Sisterhood of Martha and Mary, desperate to raise funds to keep her sanctuary and the people who rely on it safe.

Princess Alice wasn't living in the convent in 1967, but had her own home away from the order. Likewise, she was far from the vulnerable, abandoned figure that *The Crown* would have us believe: she actually took up residence in the Palace of Athens after the coup. But where's the drama in that? And this episode is all about the drama.

Prince Philip, meanwhile, did make an appearance on *Meet the Press* in America, in which he bemoaned the financial situation of the royal family. Though the episode is depicted as taking place in 1967, he was a guest on the programme in 1969. This television appearance, however, is pivotal in *The Crown* because it catches the eye of John Armstrong, ace *Guardian* reporter. Fictional *Guardian* reporter, more to the point. Fictional or slightly massaged media appearances are a theme in *Bubbikins*, from *Meet the Press* to the documentary that the family are shown filming throughout this episode. That documentary was in fact shot in 1968 and eventually became *Royal Family*, a rather infamous PR damp squib.

When news reaches England that Princess Alice is in danger in Athens, the queen immediately suggests that she should be brought to England, much to Philip's disgust. He simply will not acknowledge his mother, intent as he is on blaming her for the unhappy childhood he endured whilst she languished in a sanatorium. We've already seen this at some length in season two, but we get some flashback of grasping hands to crassly denote madness and a sobbing young Philip, just for good measure. The duke refuses to allow Alice to come to England, but Elizabeth overrules him and summons her to Buckingham Palace. It's super dramatic, but it's not super true. Philip was actually the driving force behind efforts to ensure the safety of his mother after the coup in Athens. It was he who invited Princess Alice to the palace, not his wife.

Equally facile is the depiction of Princess Alice as a wide-eyed innocent, bemused by the splendour in which she finds herself and utterly unfamiliar with her son's family. In reality, she had made regular trips to the United Kingdom in the decades after the Duke of Edinburgh married the queen and knew her grandchildren well; she was certainly no stranger to palace life. Equally fictional is the interview that Princess Anne is supposed to give to John Armstrong of *The Guardian*, which Princess Alice ends up undertaking instead. In *Bubbikins*, this accidental media coup totally transforms the royal family's reputation with the public and press alike, as well as Philip's relationship with his mother: in reality, there was no Armstrong, and there was no interview. It hardly needs to be said that there was no *Guardian* headline lionising Princess Alice as a saint either.

So to *Royal Family*, the documentary that the family are so horrified with upon its television premiere. In reality, the queen saw and approved the finished programme ahead of its airing in June 1969. There's no chance whatsoever she wouldn't have seen it until it aired and let herself be caught on the hop like as *Bubbikins* imagines. What's intriguing is the complete absence of Prince Charles in any of the scenes regarding the documentary, because he was certainly front and centre in the real thing. In addition, nobody tore the broadcast to shreds in the press and it certainly didn't leave the monarchy tottering; at worst, some journalists found it a tad dull.

Our fictional queen is shown shutting down the documentary forever, banning it from being screened overseas and rendering it as good as lost. In actuality it was shown on television abroad and is available online today, albeit unofficially. It has never been officially shown in public since the 1970s, but the queen didn't try to erase it from the public consciousness. Except in *The Crown*. And that, as they say, is that.

3.5 Coup

The Crown

In 1967, Elizabeth and Porchey tour France and America on a fact-finding mission to indulge their shared love of racehorses. During their absence, Harold Wilson devalues the pound and finds himself the target of a coup led by media baron Cecil Harmsworth King and Lord Mountbatten. When Wilson shares his suspicions with the queen, she tears Mountbatten off a strip for daring to meddle in political affairs.

The Truth

If you're keen on good history, then it's fair to say that *Coup* really ain't for you. In fact, in a series rife with tangles, confusions and fiction, this episode really goes to town. And that's saying something.

In *Aberfan*, Harold Wilson's spin doctors turned the public's search for a scapegoat against the queen herself. In *Coup*, the embattled cabinet decide to distract a public that has fallen out of love with the Labour government by throwing them Lord Mountbatten instead. As Chief of the Defence Staff since 1959, Mountbatten was ripe to be taken down a peg or two and Defence Secretary Denis Healey, under advice from senior officials, decided in 1965 that Mountbatten's tenure should not be renewed. In reality, it was he who told the earl that his career as Chief was over, but *The Crown* has Harold Wilson wield the executioner's sword. This, of course, gives Mountbatten a reason to hate Wilson and Labour, whereas he actually accepted the decision with his usual pragmatism.

Of course, the departure of Mountbatten was really marked by an eyepopping ceremony, but the fictional long walk is a rather sorry affair. Stalking out through a crowd of awkward and besuited young chaps who can't look him in the eye, an aide carrying his retirement cake and another carrying his portrait bringing up the rear, Mountbatten's departure in *The Crown* has a whiff of the middle manager waiting for his carriage clock. The real ceremony, attended by the earl's family and a full military band, was a far less low-key and sorry affair.

The Crown is at pains to depict Mountbatten as a natural and passionate hater of all that Labour stands for, as well as the sort of unfeeling brute of a brother who has deserted his sister, the ailing and elderly Princess Alice. As we know from the fictional headline in the last episode, Alice is an undisputed royal angel in human form, so it's only natural that her ambitious and scheming sibling should turn his back on her. But guess what? It's make believe. Alice and Mountbatten saw each other often both before and after her relocation to England and she was a regular visitor to his Broadlands home. Likewise, Mountbatten was anything but the true blue Tory you might suspect. He supported the Labour government so vocally that courtiers scoffed at his "Pinko" credentials.

Though the timeline is skewed as ever, the real problems arise with the depiction of the queen gadding about on an equestrian jolly whilst the government stands on the edge of a coup led by Mountbatten. The episode tells us that the pound has just been devalued, which means it must be November 1967, a time when Her Majesty was certainly in the country rather than jetting off to France to gaze wistfully at racehorses with Porchey.

Whilst she is away, media and banking baron Cecil Harmsworth King convenes a meeting of sinister men in suits. They have concocted a plan to oust Wilson, kick out the Labour government and install Mountbatten as a new PM, utilising the queen's special powers to do so. This might seem like something that has to be made up, but it does have some basis in reality. In 1968, King did indeed approach Mountbatten with such an offer, but it obviously came to nothing. However, whilst sources differ on whether Mountbatten was horrified or tempted by the idea, *Coup* naturally finds him rather keen on it. He's busy scheming about how best to inveigle Her Majesty into his devious plans when a panicking Wilson telephones Elizabeth during her jaunt to Kentucky and asks her to come home and put her in-law straight. None of this happened. Especially not Kentucky, a place she didn't visit until the 1980s.

The plans for a coup faded into nothing almost before they had been drawn up, regardless of Mountbatten's true feelings about them. This episode manages to get an hour or so of telly out of it, but little of it has any basis in fact.

3.6 Tywysog Cymru

The Crown

Prince Charles has finally begun to flourish, having discovered a passion for theatrical pursuits whilst studying at Cambridge. He is keen to follow Wilson's suggestion to get to know Wales, since he is to become its prince. As tensions rise, Charles immerses himself in Welsh culture and language of Wales before he is invested as Prince of Wales.

Charles befriends his tutor, Tedi Millward, and becomes interested in the cause of Welsh nationalism, but his decision to make a speech about the issue angers his mother. When he argues that he must be allowed to express himself without losing her affection, she tells him that such things don't matter: instead, Charles should tamp down his personal opinions, master his emotions and serve the Crown.

The Truth

After *Coup*'s mix of fact and fiction, we're heading off to Wales again for another mix of fact and fiction, this time in the company of Prince Charles. Remember him? It's been a while since we saw Charles and by 1968 he's a young man, studying at Cambridge and falling in love with amateur theatricals as a member of Footlights. Charles is also preparing for a rather more serious bit of theatre: his investiture as Prince of Wales. Curiously though, despite scenes of the cabinet meeting with the curmudgeonly Duke of Norfolk and other courtiers who will plan the investiture, there's no sign of Lord Snowdon. Princess Margaret's husband was a driving force on the planning committee, but he's nowhere to be seen in this episode despite his central role and eye-catching outfit in the real thing. Intriguingly, the Snowdons were already the subject of divorce speculation at this point, so it's doubly frustrating to see no sign of Tony and only the barest glimpse of Margaret.

Whilst plans for Prince Charles to spend an undergraduate term in Aberystwyth preparing for his investiture were actually laid down long before he enrolled at Cambridge, *The Crown* presents things a little differently. The details of the visit were made in agreement with Charles by a committee that included his mother and father as well as Prime Minister Harold Wilson. In *Tywysog Cymru*, however, Wilson asks the queen to send Charles to Wales on a whim, to quell Welsh nationalist protests. Taken entirely by surprise, Charles is bitterly disappointed to learn that he will have to leave Cambridge for a term, much to the disinterest of his stone-faced parents. Of course, no such scenes ever occurred; Charles knew well in advance that he would be visiting Wales during his studies.

Also taken by surprise is Tedi Millward, the tutor who will be responsible for Charles during his sojourn in Wales. Whilst it's true that Millward had his reservations about the whole affair, he was aware of his responsibilities for a long time before he welcomed Prince Charles to Aberystwyth. Whilst *Tywysog Cymru* plays fast and loose with much of the history, though, it oddly chooses to ignore a couple of very dramatic incidents that did accompany Charles's arrival in Wales. The show hints at unrest but fails to dramatise an incident in 1968 when protestors smoke bombed the prince's car. No forlorn figure cowering in a chauffeur-driven vehicle, he was actually in his own sporty number and didn't seem remotely fazed. It also has nothing to say about an interview Charles gave in which he discussed the possibility of protests upon his arrival. Perhaps the latter would have made the prince look a little too forthright; *The Crown* is fond of depicting him as an awkward, repressed and resentful figure in the shadow of his parents. He'll have to wait a while yet before he's allowed to blossom.

Academic Edward "Tedi" Millward gets off fairly lightly when it comes to accuracy; as *Tywysog Cymru* depicts, Charles wasn't addressed by his royal titles at university, but was instead referred to as Mr Windsor. Likewise, Millward did discuss Welsh nationalism with the prince. It was he who encouraged his charge to learn Welsh in the university's language lab, just as viewers saw. Charles threw himself into learning both the history and the tongue of Wales; indeed, he has often spoken of how deeply he cherishes the country and he speaks its language fluently today. Where things take a swerve is in the scenes of the lonely prince visiting Millward's home and slowly being welcomed into the family without any airs and graces. In the simple but cosy surroundings he finds a warmth and affection that has been lacking in his own upbringing; sadly, no such nurturing visit to chez Millward actually happened.

Never a show to shy away from conflict, *The Crown* depicts Prince Charles amending the speech he will give at his investiture to make some heartfelt political and personal points: naturally, this angers his mother. Whilst the prince did indeed make some changes, none were in anyway controversial unless you find a joke about *The Goon Show* particularly upsetting. Also, he delivered his speech in both Welsh and English, not only Welsh, as depicted here. There was certainly no deliberate attempt to antagonise his parents by making sure they couldn't understand a word he said. Scenes of the prince arriving back in Windsor only to find the castle echoing and empty, however, are true. What's less accurate is that Charles and the queen ended his Welsh sojourn with a furious disagreement about the old guard versus the new. If you sniff a theme, you'd be right.

As *Tywysog Cymru* ends, Morgan lathers on the symbolism when a whey-faced Charles steps out on stage in character as Richard II. Pregnant with meaning though the hollow crown might be, Charles never actually played the part. But it drives the point home.

3.7 Moondust

The Crown

Following the death of his mother, Princess Alice, Prince Philip is once again dissatisfied with his lot and begins to brood on how his life might have been different. When he is offered a chance to meet Apollo astronauts Neil Armstrong, Michael Collins and Buzz Aldrin during their celebration tour, the duke hopes that their cosmic insight might somehow help him in his search for a meaning to his life. Instead, he finds that they are more fascinated by his role as a royal than by their own experiences in space.

As he continues his quest for a universal truth, Philip is invited by the new Dean of Windsor, Robin Woods, to attend a religious academy that he has established at Windsor. Philip admits to the group that he has lost his faith and, with their compassion and support, he sets about finding it again.

The Truth

It is July 1969 and the Duke of Edinburgh and Queen Elizabeth are watching a press conference by the astronauts who will soon head to the moon, Philip has important things on his mind. But in all honesty, when doesn't he? Whilst the queen celebrates having been asked to send a message into space, her husband is wondering about faith and eternity. If you've missed Prince Philip being angsty about nothing in particular, then fear not, because normal service is resumed: *Moondust* sees Philip no longer angsting about his romantic life, his lack of purpose or his wife's rank, but something far more eternal. He wants to discover nothing less than the meaning of life itself.

The following morning, a bored Philip is counting the minutes in his Windsor pew as he waits for the long-serving Dean of Windsor, Eric Hamilton, to finish his sermon. Once he's safely out of the chapel, the duke tells his wife that, after eighteen years of Hamilton, the time has come to seek a brand new Dean, preferably one who won't be so dull. Ouch. But whilst it's true that the Dean of Windsor was replaced in the 1960s, Hamilton actually went in 1962: years before the moon landing took place. And he didn't go because the Duke of Edinburgh thought he was boring, but because he died.

As the royal family gathers to watch the launch of Apollo 11, Philip broods. In fact, he broods himself into an entirely fictional and frankly bizarre obsession with the moon, which is only interrupted by the arrival of Robin Woods, the new Dean of Windsor. Woods is seeking the duke's permission to establish a new centre at Windsor that will support priests who are suffering crises of faith. Philip mocks the idea, but our angsty duke would, wouldn't he?

In fact, Robin Woods and Prince Philip did indeed work together to establish St George's House, except they did so in 1966. Nor is the welcoming establishment reserved for clergy, but is instead open to all. The Duke of Edinburgh didn't become unhealthily obsessed with the moon landings until he spiralled into self-destructive misery, which eventually resulted in him losing his religious faith altogether. Nor was his fictional loss of faith exacerbated by the death of his mother, since she passed away in December 1969, months after man first walked on the moon. Whether the Duke of Edinburgh had a crisis of faith we cannot say, but I find it unlikely. This episode, for better or worse, is a lot more fiction than fact.

The centre of *Moondust* is Philip's personal audience with the three astronauts, whom he hopes will bestow on him some sort of deep eternal insight, thus affording him just a glimpse of the new horizons they have been privileged to see firsthand. Instead, they are dazzled by his celebrity and rank and have plenty of questions of their own, all of them about what life is like for the Duke of Edinburgh. Philip is disillusioned and disappointed: he had been hoping for more. It has to be said that the depiction of the crew of Apollo 11 is exceptionally odd; to a man, they're shown to be dull, lacking in curiosity and obsessed with mundanities. In fact, these accomplished and intelligent men who had been handpicked to undertake a mission that would make history. So why on earth are they depicted as wide-eyed hayseeds?

Whilst the queen and Duke of Edinburgh did indeed meet the crew of Apollo 11, they did so together at an audience that lasted for 45 minutes, rather than the private 15 minute powwow with the duke depicted here. The crew spoke warmly about the queen's fascination with and knowledge of their mission, but they made no comment on Philip's role in the conversation. In *Moondust*, however, he is the centre of attention. Plus ça change.

Eventually, Philip's search for meaning takes him to St George's House, the very support establishment he had scoffed at when Robin Woods first mooted the idea. With the help of the new friends, he finds there, the Duke of Edinburgh's faith is renewed and, happily for the fictional Philip, peace is restored at the palace.

3.8 Dangling Man

The Crown

Prince Charles has found himself caught not in a love triangle, but a love rectangle, as he is dating Camilla Shand, who is also dating Andrew Parker Bowles…, who is dating Princess Anne.

For Queen Elizabeth, meanwhile, it is a time for goodbyes as she visits the dying Duke of Windsor, who seeks her forgiveness for his past wrongs. As a final act, the duke gives his niece the letters which he has received from Prince Charles, in which he pours out his heart to his black sheep great uncle.

Meanwhile, at Downing Street, it's all change again: Wilson is out of office and Edward Heath is unpacking his piano.

The Truth

It's been a while since we saw the Duke of Windsor, but he's back. And, just like his brother in the very first moments of *The Crown*, he's coughing up blood. *Dangling Man* does all kinds of things to the timeline, but for what it's worth, this is how it unfolded in real life. In 1969, the Duke of Windsor gave a television interview that was broadcast the following year, in 1970. A year after that, in 1971, Prince Charles met the abdicated king for the first and only time. Soon afterwards, the Duke of Windsor fell ill. When and if he learned that his condition was terminal throat cancer is not public knowledge.

Dangling Man covers most of these events after a fashion, though in a completely different order. The duke falls ill in 1970 and receives a terminal diagnosis with Wallis at his side; this didn't happen. It must be 1970, because we see Ted Heath supplant Harold Wilson at Downing Street, an event which took place that summer. However, on planet *Crown,* Michael Adeane has retired from the queen's service in favour of Martin Charteris, which happened two years later. So far, so muddled. Only once the Duke of Windsor knows he is dying does he contrive to film his BBC interview, after which Prince Charles seeks permission to visit his uncle at his French home. Whilst all of this is going on, Andrew Parker Bowles and Camilla Shand's on and off romance is definitely off; as a result,

Andrew starts dating Princess Anne and Camilla starts dating Prince Charles, after meeting him at a polo match. It's the start of the aforementioned love rectangle, with various people dating various royals, sometimes concurrently.

Once again, this is timeline massaging for the sake of drama. though Camilla and Andrew certainly were very much on-again-off-again, they were comprehensively off when each took up with their own royal paramour. There was no crossover in the dating, and no question of the slightly icky sibling rivalry that's in evidence here. In fact, whilst Camilla and Charles were friends, they didn't begin their relationship until 1972, after the death of the Duke of Windsor. He is still alive in this episode as they begin to get serious. Though Charles and Camilla share a cute dinner and a practical joke on the night the duke's interview is broadcast, it was actually televised months before they had even met.

Where the episode does stray almost accidentally into fact is in Mountbatten's advice to Charles that he is too young to settle down. In fact, Dickie wrote to his great nephew in 1974 and encouraged him to sow his wild oats before marriage, then find an inexperienced innocent young lady with whom to tie the knot and produce an heir. And we all know how that turned out.

When news reaches the queen that the Duke of Windsor is on his deathbed, she drops everything to rush to his side, catching the duke and his wife off guard. In fact, that visit had been planned for months, and was due to take place during an official trip Her Majesty was making to France. Whilst the queen actually arrived with the Duke of Edinburgh and Prince Charles, this episode shows her making the visit to her pitifully weak uncle alone.

There is a moment in *Dangling Man* when the Duke of Windsor insists on standing from his wheelchair to greet Elizabeth with due deference, despite his infirmity; this small but significant gesture did take place. To the end, the duke wished to show proper respect to Her Majesty the Queen. What we cannot know is whether uncle David received letters from Prince Charles which spoke rapturously of Camilla and hinted that things might have been better had the abdicated king retained the crown, with Wallis as his queen. The drama!

Despite the duke's troublesome nature and scandalous past, though, Charles did foster a relationship with his uncle at Mountbatten's urging.

The prince met him once at a party the Windsors were throwing in Paris but it was an experience that the idealistic Prince of Wales found dispiriting. What was discussed in the letters the two men exchanged must remain a secret: when Mountbatten arranged for the Duke of Windsor's correspondence to be catalogued after his death, no such letters were included amongst the papers.

Moments before the fictional Duke of Windsor takes his last breath with the duchess at his side, his pet pug jumps from the bed. It's an incident that is heavy with meaning and one that is taken from the historical record. Wallis, however, was not at her husband's bedside at the moment of his death. She was actually in bed; whether alone or with someone else will depend on whose version of events you choose to believe.

3.9 Imbroglio

The Crown

The country is reeling from the impact of the miners' strike, which has resulted in electricity being rationed. As Charles embarks on his military training at Dartmouth, Lord Mountbatten and the Queen Mother scheme to break up his relationship with Camilla by sending the prince abroad for months.

The Queen Mother receives the Shand and Parker Bowles parents and succeeds in brokering a marriage between their two offspring, which she hopes will stymy the relationship between Charles and Camilla once and for all.

The Truth

A week after the Duke of Windsor dies, he is brought home to Windsor to be laid to rest. Dignified in her grief, his widow comes face to face with the royal family at the funeral, for what all hope will be the last time. At the Windsor Castle gathering that follows, we are served several dollops of meaningful conversation as the production draws frankly clumsy parallels between Charles and Camilla's relationship and that of the Duke and Duchess of Windsor: it must have been too juicy to resist for the production team. Recognising her late husband's spirit in the young Prince of Wales, Wallis warns him to beware of his family, who are looking on vulture-like in a suitably sinister fashion. The Firm, indeed.

In case you failed to be bowled over by the similarities, Camilla and Wallis lock eyes as the widow departs Windsor for the last time, leaving Miss Shand a little spooked by the whole affair. Yet the composed, wise Mrs Simpson here is a world away from the real thing; the duchess was plunged into deep shock at the death of the duke and left for Paris in the company of her personal physician immediately after the funeral service at Windsor. She was reportedly barely aware of what was happening around her, so great was her sorrow.

Timeline-wise, there is more confusion as Ted Heath visits the queen to discuss the ongoing miners' strike, which is actuality had ended months before the death of the Duke of Windsor. Though Heath is one of the less characterised politicians in *The Crown*, scenes of him playing the piano and whispers about his bachelorhood are reflective of both his musical talent and the gossip around his unmarried status. Whether the Duke of Edinburgh was the one spreading that gossip is rather more questionable.

Meanwhile, Prince Charles is off training with the Royal Navy at Dartmouth. It's another timeline fudge but whilst he's away, he decides that he's fallen in love with Camilla. And Lord Mountbatten is not happy. It's here things take another odd turn: Mountbatten and the Queen Mother were never close at all, but in *Imbroglio* they morph into some kind of Bond villain double act and cook up a plot to tear our star-crossed lovers apart. Dickie will see to it that Charles is sent away to a far-flung naval outpost, whilst the Queen Mother will take care of Camilla. Given the sinister manner in which they discuss the conspiracy by lamplight, whether "taking care" translates as dropping her into a concealed piranha tank has yet to be seen.

In *Imbroglio*, Lord Mountbatten cruelly engineers a nine month posting for Charles aboard the destroyer *Norfolk*, a posting that was actually arranged months before the prince even began his training, but that's just the start of the scheming. The Queen Mother has barely made an impact in this season, but now she's up off the sofa and away from the television with a vengeance. In the midst of a blackout she summons the Parker Bowles and Shand parents to visit her at Clarence House, where she brokers a marriage. It's so ridiculous that I wish it was true. Just imagine a supervillain pairing of Dickie and the Queen Mum. Wouldn't that be delicious?

When Charles protests to his mother that someone is conspiring against him, the queen summons our villains and gives them a firm telling off. However, as they explain their motives, her resolve begins to weaken. Faced with the prospect of commoner Camilla as a possible Princess of Wales, the queen wonders if perhaps her mother might have a point. The die is cast and the ramifications will rumble on for decades.

Camilla decides to go along with the path of least resistance and accepts a proposal from Andrew Parker Bowles, despite heavy hints from the scriptwriters that she truly loves Prince Charles. This is one moment that is hard to pin down, but it seems that Camilla's friends had been anticipating a proposal from the prince when the couple visited Broadlands in December 1972. When none came, the affair fizzled and Andrew was soon back on the scene, ready to woo his future wife anew. When Charles learned of the engagement, he was upset but accepting of his fate: Camilla really did love Andrew at the time of their marriage, whatever *Imbroglio* seems to intimate about plot and counterplot. Once more for those at the back, there was no conspiracy by the Queen Mother and Mountbatten.

If only. I'd have been all over that franchise.

3.10 Cri de Coeur

The Crown

Miserable in her collapsing marriage, Margaret begins an affair with the much younger Roddy Llewellyn. However, when newspapers publish photographs of the couple in the Caribbean, the queen summons them home to England.

Heartbroken and feeling trapped, Margaret attempts suicide. As Queen Elizabeth prepares for her Silver Jubilee in 1977, she and her sister finally reconcile.

The Truth

It's been a while since we saw a dead man rising from the grave in *The Crown*, but as the show prepares to close the season, we're treated to another resurrection. Spare a thought for the Duke of Gloucester, who is happily holding court at Princess Margaret's August 1974 birthday party and later preparing to celebrate the queen's jubilee in 1977. He wasn't about to let the fact that he died in June 1974 slow him down.

But still, here we go with *Cri de Coeur*.

It is 1974, a year that saw two General Elections heralded the return of Harold Wilson to number 10. As Lord Snowdon and his lover, Lucy Lindsay-Hogg (later the second Mrs Armstrong-Jones) set off for a weekend of amour, they little realised that they have been spotted by Princess Margaret's lady-in-waiting. Margaret, sleeping until noon, drunk at breakfast and wearing a suitably wild look, is heartbroken to learn that her husband has betrayed her. With divorce against her faith, the princess grows ever more furious as her family, led by the Queen Mother, loudly sing the praises of the errant and absent Snowdon at her birthday party. It's like a Windsor version of *Eastenders*. Timeline-wise, it's worth noting that neither of the General Elections that year took place anywhere near Margaret's birthday.

Whilst attending a house party with her eagle-eyed lady-in-waiting Anne Tennant, Margaret's roving eye is caught by gardener Roddy Llewelyn. Enchanted by the younger man's free-spirited nature, she plunges into her first extra-marital affair. In fact, she had actually already had several affairs before this, but *The Crown* wants us to believe that Margaret was driven to stray by Snowdon's neglect. Just as Morgan fuddled the truth regarding her refusal to step out of the line of succession to marry Peter Townsend, he once again chooses to give the princess the benefit of a very substantial bit of doubt. As a sidenote, she was introduced to Roddy by the Tennants in 1973, not 1974 as depicted here.

As Snowdon gets busy okaying merch for the queen's forthcoming Silver Jubilee, Margaret and Roddy are off for a jolly on the Tennants' island of Mustique. This happened in February 1974, and *Cri de Coeur* suggests the trip was as just the tonic Margaret needed to pep her up. However, little known to the couple, a photographer is papping them as Roddy lathers sun cream all over his lover. This is kind of how the affair got out, though it was actually in 1976, and there was no sun lotion: the couple simply sat on the same stretch of beach and kept their hands resolutely to themselves. Perhaps this might've seemed a bit chaste for modern audiences though, hence the hands-on dramatic license to drive home the point that this was a Major Scandal.

Summoned home to England to face the music, Margaret is confronted by her furious husband about her humiliating and very public betrayal. Though Tony was in Australia when the photographs were published, in *Cri de Coeur* he is at home and filled with puppyish excitement at the thought of Jubilee mugs, so Margaret's roll in the sand with Roddy really punctures his balloon. Similarly punctured is the queen, when she receives Wilson's early retirement. Her Majesty thought very highly of Harold Wilson and was undoubtedly genuinely sorry to learn of his premature departure, which was indeed due to the onset of Alzheimer's disease, just as this episode depicts. Whether he disclosed his diagnosis to her when he resigned we cannot know, but it is significant that she attended a formal farewell dinner for Wilson, the first such royal gesture for a departing PM since Churchill.

No sooner has Wilson left the palace than Elizabeth receives another blow: Margaret has taken an overdose of sleeping pills. This is a reflection of something that sort of happened, when the princess took a handful of tablets whilst holidaying on Mustique in 1974. It was long before the affair was revealed, however, and a confused Roddy had fled overseas in order to try and work out his feelings for the mercurial princess, plunging her into depression. She was warring with Snowdon at the time and even asked her husband to leave their home, but the split wasn't brought about by the publicity surrounding her affair with Llewelyn. The marriage was always tumultuous.

As the queen and Margaret renew their loving friendship, Tony is off the scene for good. It's dramatic but fictional: the Snowdons didn't divorce until 1978 and even continued to see one another off and on for a couple more years. In addition, whilst *The Crown* depicts a violent argument that severed their connection forever, they remained good friends even after their divorce. The series concludes with a grim-faced queen climbing into her carriage alone to celebrate the Jubilee; she appears to have forgotten the Duke of Edinburgh, who in reality joined her on the journey through cheering crowds on 7 June 1977. And she did manage to crack a smile, unlike our fictionalised monarch.

If this episode belongs to Margaret, once again we've seen another significant female character silenced. During the period covered by

Cri de Coeur, Princess Anne married Mark Phillips and even managed to evade a kidnap attempt, fighting off her would-be assailant with a much-celebrated "not bloody likely", before going on to train for the Olympic Games. The omission of her wedding and especially her kidnapping feels really unforgiveable in a season that gave a whole episode over to the Duke of Edinburgh's fictional mooning after the moon. It's a sadly missed opportunity to shine a much-deserved spotlight on the Princess Royal.

❧ SEASON 4 ❧

4.1 Gold Stick

The Crown

In the first episode of the new season, relations are tense between Princess Anne and her husband, Mark. Elsewhere, Prince Charles has a fateful first meeting with his girlfriend's younger sister and the IRA target Lord Mountbatten, plunging the royal family into grief.

At Downing Street, meanwhile, Margaret Thatcher is beginning her first term as prime minister.

The Truth

It's all change once more as *The Crown* launches into its hotly anticipated fourth season, with audiences poised to finally meet a certain Lady Diana Spencer.

First, the easy part. Margaret Thatcher did indeed come to power in 1979 and she did indeed do her own ironing; she was also known around the palace for her absurdly low curtsies. Three ticks for accuracy there. Less accurate is the depiction of the relationship that existed between Elizabeth II and Margaret Thatcher. Anything but timid on the floor of the House of Commons, meeting the queen was one of the few experiences that tended to quail Mrs Thatcher. But that isn't how *The Crown* presents her. Instead she is as confident, self-assured and forthright with the monarch as she is around her own dinner table. She's never afraid of sharing her opinion with Elizabeth in *the* Crown, whereas in reality she found their early encounters nerve-wracking and even once she was settled into the role, she was always deferential

88

and awestruck. It's also worth mentioning the moment when the Duke of Edinburgh scoffs at Thatcher's scientific training too, dismissive as he is at the idea of having a woman in Downing Street. Of course, Prince Philip's real reaction to Thatcher's election and past history is unknown, but given his widely documented interest in science, his mocking her for studying chemistry seems like a bit of a reach. It's also a surprise to see the ongoing presence of Martin Charteris in the queen's service: he had retired and been succeeded by Philip Moore by this point.

The Prince of Wales's love life was famously studded with glamorous names and members of the country set. Despite this, several of the women referred to as ex-girlfriends in this episode had yet to date him when it takes place. One of those country set girls who was very definitely in the prince's little black book at this point though was Lady Sarah Spencer, the elder sister of Lady Diana.

Also inaccurate is the depiction of Prince Charles meeting Lady Diana in 1979, whilst he's both dating her sister and secretly seeing the now-married Camilla on the side. The Spencers and the Windsors had known each other for years; Diana's grandmothers were ladies-in-waiting to the Queen Mother and young Diana used to play with Charles's brothers at Sandringham in childhood, but the couple actually met for the first time in 1977, when Lady Diana was 16. I'm sorry to say that she wasn't wafting masked and sylph-like through potted plants at the time, as *The Crown* suggests: instead, they were introduced at a grouse shoot at Althorp, the Spencer family seat. Her nickname really was Duch, short for Duchess, though.

The real drama in *Gold Stick*, of course, comes with the murder of Lord Mountbatten at the hands of the IRA. Mountbatten was known to spend summers at Classiebawn Castle in County Sligo, which lay only a handful of miles from the border with Northern Ireland. At the time, the Troubles were a political flashpoint and IRA activity was at its height; there had even been plans for an IRA sniper to kill Mountbatten in 1978, but bad weather forced the cancellation of the plot.

On 27 August 1979, Mountbatten went fishing with members of his family, unaware that the IRA had planted a remote-controlled bomb aboard their vessel, *Shadow V*. As the boat sailed out of Mullaghmore, the device was detonated. Mountbatten and his grandson were killed, as was a teenaged crewmember. The earl's daughter, son-in-law, and another grandson were badly injured, whilst Doreen, Dowager Lady Brabourne, the mother of Mountbatten's son-in-law, died the following day. The attack sent shockwaves around the world and plunged the royal family into mourning. However, scenes depicting Mrs Thatcher leaving a cabinet meeting to receive news of the bombing are sheer fiction: Mountbatten died on a Bank Holiday Monday in the middle of the Parliamentary recess.

As messages of condolence poured in from around the world, the IRA issued a statement in which they claimed responsibility for the murder. By this time, a man named Thomas McMahon was already in custody, having been arrested at a checkpoint on suspicion of possessing a stolen vehicle hours before the bomb that killed Mountbatten was detonated. He was convicted of the killing on the strength of forensic evidence in 1979 and remained in prison until 1998, when he was released under the terms of the Good Friday Agreement.

In *Gold Stick*, one of Mountbatten's last actions before his death is to write a loving but stern letter to Prince Charles, in which he admonishes him for his behaviour and tells him to do better. The Prince of Wales receives the letter in the aftermath of his beloved uncle's death and it has a profound impact on him. In reality, no such letter was written, though it is true that Prince Charles, who had viewed Mountbatten as an honorary grandfather, was hit particularly hard by his loss. Although the letter is fictional, Mountbatten's affectionate address to Charles of "honorary grandson" is real, as is Charles's devastation at his great uncle's violent death.

The year after Mountbatten's murder, as her sister Lady Sarah prepared for her own wedding, Diana approached Charles to offer her condolences on Dickie's death. In *The Crown* it's depicted a sweet moment of true emotional connection between the couple, but in real life, Diana confided in her friends that Charles received her condolences then immediately moved in for a snog, much to her amused disgust. Of course, that doesn't fit with the lovelorn television prince, so thankfully there's no pouncing to be seen. Incidentally, Charles's relationship with Lady Sarah Spencer was never particularly serious and there was no suggestion that he was intending to marry her, nor would he have needed to ask her permission to date Diana. In *Gold Stick*, however, as *The Crown* gears up for the tumultuous melodrama of the marriage of Charles and Diana, he gets on the blower and asks Lady Sarah for her blessing to take her sister out. She says yes and the rest, as we know, is history.

4.2 The Balmoral Test

The Crown

As Charles starts dating the seemingly perfect Lady Diana, Margaret and Denis Thatcher are gearing up for their first visit to Balmoral. Despite knowing that they will be forced to endure the "Balmoral test" to see if they fit in, they nevertheless fail miserably and use government business as an excuse to escape back to London. When a lovesick Charles seeks Camilla's advice regarding Diana, she tells him to see where the relationship goes and wishes them well.

During her own visit to Balmoral, Diana passes the test with flying colours and the royal family identifies her as a potential Princess of Wales, despite Charles's doubts. Tired of challenges from her own colleagues, Mrs Thatcher culls her opponents in a Cabinet reshuffle, proving herself to be a formidable foe.

The Truth

One thing I'll note before we dive in: in *The Crown*'s world, political wives don't say much. Political husbands, however, are fully-fledged characters with much to offer in the way of insight and spousal support. So not just nice hats and arm holding, then.

Anyway. Along with some fairly heavy-handed symbolic blood sports, *The Balmoral Test* is all about the royal family's fictional efforts to catch out their visitors and have a jolly good laugh at their expense. Though *the Balmoral Test* gives the Windsors a chance to be thoroughly ghoulish and make the Thatchers feel like uncultured oafs in their presence, the royal family's visitors have never had anything but nice things to say. Now, you might say that visitors to the royal household are bound to say that, but it's unlikely that the family would go out of their way to be quite as monstrous as this episode suggests. Until we're told otherwise, we'll have to chalk this house of horrors up as fiction.

It's also unlikely the Thatchers would commit quite as many serious social faux pas as *The Balmoral Test* suggests, from dressing for dinner far too early to going stalking in the Highlands in a power suit and court shoes. Nor did the couple flee for London on a spurious excuse, but saw out the entire stay as scheduled. It's unthinkable that Thatcher, who was immensely deferential to the monarch, would've run out on her. Rumour has it, however, that Thatcher loathed the visits to Balmoral and used to deliberately take the wrong shoes just so she had an excuse not to go out yomping. She was outmanoeuvred by canny staff, who made sure to have a pair of wellies on hand for her to borrow.

In *The Crown* universe, time is elastic, hence Charles takes Diana to the opera at roughly the same time as the Thatchers visit Balmoral, a jaunt which is followed shortly by Diana's own Balmoral debut. In fact, Charles and Diana went to the opera and Diana subsequently visited the Highland bolthole in 1980, the year after the Thatchers' first stay.

When Diana visited Balmoral for the first time, she was on her third date with the Prince of Wales and she didn't actually stay in the castle at all. Rather, she lodged with her sister and brother-in-law, who kept a cottage on the estate. Charles would collect Diana every morning and they would spend the day together, though whether that included her spotting a heavily symbolic stag for the adoring Prince Philip is unlikely. Diana finally stayed in the castle later that year, though the queen wasn't in residence at the time. When Diana tells the Duke of Edinburgh that she was her sister's cleaner, though, the script is accurate. It's the little things.

In *The Balmoral Test*, Mrs Thatcher's reshuffle of her Cabinet is depicted as the moment at which she consolidates her power, but it didn't quite go down as the show suggests. There were two reshuffles in 1981 and that which we see in *The Crown* was a major purge which took place in September. However, Francis Pym certainly wasn't fired: he was moved to another office and remained a fixture of the Thatcher administration until his eventual sacking following Mrs T's second general election victory in 1983.

By the way, there really is a chair in which Queen Victoria sat at Balmoral and it really is forbidden for anybody to sit in it. Why it would therefore be placed at a desk just waiting for Margaret Thatcher to park her rump there and attract the chagrin of Princess Margaret is a mystery.

4.3 Fairytale

The Crown

After Charles pops the question, Diana flees from the paparazzi only to find herself isolated and lonely at Buckingham Palace. There she's forced to endure lessons in how to be a princess, not to mention contend with her rival, Camilla. Has the princess-to-be made a terrible mistake?

The Truth

Viewers of season four of *The Crown* waited keenly for Lady Diana to arrive and when she did, they weren't disappointed. The story of the ill-fated marriage of the Prince and Princess of Wales is one that has been told and retold, dividing royal watchers into fiercely opposing camps. For Peter Morgan, it must've been a gift. The most hotly anticipated royal wedding in years brought with it so much behind the scenes drama that one wonders how much fictional excitement needed to be added. Surprisingly, the dramatisation of the romance and engagement of Charles and Diana isn't as far from the truth as some other events we've seen. As the years pass, that won't always be the case.

Diana's Mini Metro will be instantly familiar to anyone who has seen the early paparazzi shots of the young nursery school teacher who had apparently captured the heart of the heir to the throne. Her Sloane Ranger style, all frilly blouses and sensible knitwear, is perfectly recreated too. Diana's clothes, in keeping with most of those in *The Crown*, are just about perfect; one can only imagine what fun the wardrobe team must have had transforming her from wallflower to glamour queen as the episodes went on.

In scenes recreating the engagement announcement, her famous bluebird of happiness outfit is instantly recognisable. The blue skirt suit and blouse, purchased by then Lady Diana from Harrods, became famous across the globe when she wore them to the press call that would officially announce her engagement to the Prince of Wales. However, Diana had originally visited Belville Sassoon for an outfit, only to encounter a disinterested sales representative, who, not realising exactly

93

who the young woman was, suggested that she might find herself more at home elsewhere. Diana took her at her word and royal history was made.

The Crown hasn't always done right by its female characters, but Diana is wisely brought right to the forefront. It's a judicious move to place her centre stage and she's the nearest thing we have to an identification figure in this season. There is quite a lot this episode gets right, from the fact that Charles popped the question in the nursery to Diana choosing the most expensive engagement ring from those on offer, though she wouldn't have known the prices at the time. It wasn't an heirloom either, but a brand new rock from the collection of royal jeweller, Garrard. The cringeworthy moment when a reporter asks the couple if they are in love and Charles replies "whatever "in love" means" unfortunately also happened, in the full glare of the world's cameras. It's since become a notorious and much discussed moment in royal history.

Whilst *The Crown* does an excellent job of showing the wrench Diana must have felt when she bid farewell to her flatmates, who ironically drink a toast to the fact that she's leaving normality and anonymity behind, it is ever so slightly guilty of overegging the pudding. The world knows now that Diana found her introduction into life as a royal fiancée bewildering and *Fairytale* captures that with scenes of the lonely teenager roller-skating through Buckingham Palace. However, because the scriptwriters don't quite trust us to get the symbolism of the cavernous corridors that swallow Diana's small figure, it goes mining for drama where it really doesn't need to.

Diana did indeed leave her Earl's Court flat to live in the royal household but she actually moved into Clarence House rather than Buckingham Palace. Whilst seeing her share her new home with the Queen Mother might have offered plenty of opportunities for exactly the fish out of water narrative that this episode is all about, placing her in Buckingham Palace means we're denied any of that. The Queen Mother is once again largely absent from this season, which seems like an odd choice given the fact that she was anything but absent from Diana's early days in the royal household. Likewise, the scenes of Diana making embarrassing protocol gaffes and being schooled in etiquette by her fearsome grandmother, Lady Fermoy, are more fiction than fact. Diana didn't grow up in a normal household, but one that had close and longstanding royal ties. She simply wouldn't have needed to be given a crash course in how to behave as though she was a country bumpkin who had rolled in from nowhere. Intriguingly, it later emerged that Lady Fermoy had counselled her granddaughter against the marriage.

Lady Diana is doubtlessly the hero of this episode and in true panto style, that means we need someone to boo. That role is filled ably by Charles, who abandons his lonely fiancée to the echoing hallways of Buckingham Palace and its distant inhabitants almost as soon as the engagement is announced. In reality, whilst Charles did indeed undertake an overseas tour several weeks after the royal family toasted the engagement at dinner, he didn't duck out of the gathering to race off for foreign climes within hours, as *Fairytale* depicts.

Fairytale is the first episode of the series to deal with Diana's eating disorder, as she steals down to the kitchen alone to find comfort in food, before making herself vomit. It is a pattern we see time and time again and one that we now know mirrors the princess's very real struggle with bulimia. What is perhaps surprising is that scriptwriters didn't include an occasion that Diana herself related and which she blamed for exacerbating her struggles. She recalled that, during an embrace, Prince Charles put his hand on her waist and commented that she was getting chubby. This would've seemed like a gift to production, but it isn't depicted at all.

One scene that you'd be forgiven for thinking had to have been invented by the scriptwriters is the excruciatingly awkward lunch between Diana and Camilla. Well, believe it or not, it happened, though it happened after the wedding, not before. It wasn't their first meeting as the script suggests, but though the two women moved in similar sets, they had never been close. And yes, it really was at a restaurant called Ménage à Trois that bizarrely tried to please female clients by removing all main courses from the menu. The intention behind the lunch was to introduce Diana to someone from outside the stuffy palace whom Charles hoped might turn into a friend, an endeavour that turned out precisely as well as you might think, as the world was eventually to learn.

On screen, it's during this lunch that Diana realises how little she really knows about her fiancé and just how intimately Camilla and Charles are connected. The scene is also useful for introducing the "Fred and Gladys" nicknames that Charles and Camilla had given one another, a revelation that will come back to torment Diana and lead her to a future confrontation when she discovers that Charles has commissioned a bracelet for Camilla engraved with "GF".

We know now that both Charles and Diana were wracked with doubts about their wedding, which the episode certainly captures. We know also that Diana was unhappy at Charles's close relationship with Camilla and that the bracelet, with its seemingly incriminating engraving, was a token he gave to Camilla a few days before the wedding. However, there have been suggestions that *GF* actually alluded to another nickname, *Girl Friday*, and that Charles was simply intending to honour Camilla as the sort of friend who had been there for him through thick and thin. Intriguingly, royal insiders have also claimed that there was nothing special about Charles giving his ex-girlfriend the gift in the first place. He certainly made similar gifts of jewellery to other former girlfriends just before his wedding as a token of his esteem and affection for them.

Though the episode has Charles tell Diana that the bracelet was merely a gift between friends, he doesn't allay her fears in the obvious way, by admitting that he has sent similar gifts to a whole host of exes. Instead, he tries to comfort his fiancée by giving her a gold signet ring in the moments before a tense wedding rehearsal. This is a reference to the signet ring that Charles sent to Diana at Clarence House on the night before their marriage, an evening when both parties were anxiously wondering just what they'd let themselves in for

Just as the series didn't show the exchange between Charles and Diana regarding her weight, nor does it dramatise the much-discussed moment on the eve of the wedding when Charles supposedly told his fiancée that he didn't love her. This claim was made by friends of the late princess rather than Diana herself, but the scriptwriters certainly capture the impression of two people hurtling towards disaster. Indeed, viewers see Princess Margaret warn her mother, sister and brother-in-law that they should stop the wedding before it is too late. They don't, of course, despite a tense stand-off between the queen and Charles when she tells him the curious story of his own grandmother's marriage. Queen Mary, says Her Majesty, only married George V because her one true love, who just happened to be his brother, died before she could be wed to him. Well, sort of.

Mary was born in 1867 and, as the daughter of Francis, Duke of Teck, and Princess Mary Adelaide of Cambridge, was an eminently suitable bride for Prince Albert Victor, Duke of Clarence, her second cousin and the eldest son of the Prince of Wales. Queen Victoria was very fond of Mary and encouraged the marriage between the couple. Mary accepted out of duty, not because she was madly in love with her suitor, as *The Crown* would have us believe. As it happened, Mary's fiancé fell victim to the influenza pandemic just six weeks later. That meant that his younger brother, Prince George, Duke of York, was now second in line to throne behind his father, and Queen Victoria was extremely keen to find him a wife. The easiest solution was simply to switch one brother for another and marry Mary to the Duke of York instead. Remarkably, the marriage was a resounding success; the couple fell in love quickly and, rare amongst royal husbands, George was faithful to his bride.

Earlier seasons of *The Crown* have given audiences remarkable recreations of royal pomp and ceremony, including weddings, funerals and coronations, but despite or perhaps because the wedding of Charles and Diana was one of the most famous and well-covered that the world has ever seen, it doesn't merit any screentime at all. Instead, we see an apprehensive Diana in her wedding gown, dwarfed by the grandeur of Buckingham Palace as she prepares to meet her fate in front of 750 million television viewers worldwide.

4.4 Favourites

The Crown

When Mark Thatcher, the prime minister's favourite child, goes missing during the Paris-Dakar rally, Thatcher's uncharacteristic distress leads the queen to examine her relationships with her own children.

On the far side of the world, Argentina invades the Falkland Islands, whilst in England, a pregnant Diana feels trapped in her failing marriage and Charles continues to make Camilla his confidante.

The Truth

Firstly, let's deal with the Falkland Islands. In *Favourites*, British scientists clash with Argentine scrap metal workers in South Georgia, where they're shocked to discover that the bullish Argentines have graffitied the sentiment, *Las Malvinas son Argentinas*, across the abandoned whaling station that they have been dismantling despite not having the authorisation to do so. This early blow in what would become the Falklands conflict did take place, but whilst the Argentinians didn't have permits to work, nor did they scrawl graffiti across the wall. In addition, relations between the British and Argentines were cordial rather than tense and jeering as *Favourites* would have us believe. Likewise, whilst it appears that the clash in the Falklands and Mark's disappearance happened on the same day, there was actually a gap of two months between the events. With the Argentinian government keen to reclaim the islands, the Falklands conflict was destined to become one of the defining incidents of Margaret Thatcher's political career.

The disappearance of Mark Thatcher and the tensions between the PM and her daughter are true to life. Mark turned up safe and well after a massive search operation, with no idea whatsoever of the drama that his vanishing had caused, whilst his twin sister, Carol, has spoken candidly about her sometimes strained relationship with her mother. Whether Mrs T cried during her audience with the queen is a matter of conjecture, but she was certainly enormously distressed at her son's disappearance.

I think we can surmise that the queen's scheduled getting-to-know-you appointments with each of her children are a work of fiction. This episode really exists for two reasons. First is to give the Falklands conflict some screentime, because as this episode draws to a close we will see Mrs Thatcher at the pinnacle of her popularity, commanding the spotlight whilst her sovereign sits at home. Second, it drives home the point that the queen and the Duke of Edinburgh have not been successful as parents. It's something regular viewers already have seen plenty of times in preceding seasons, but *Favourites* showcases the sentiment once and for all.

During her own heart-to-heart with her mother, Princess Anne is resentful that the queen shows her horse more fondness than she shows her daughter and seems jealous both of Princess Diana's wardrobe and her relationship with the media. In fact, this really goes against what we know of the Princess Royal, who enjoyed a very close relationship with her mother. Two things Princess Anne has shown little interest in are fostering good relationships with the media, who she really did tell to "naff off", and fashion. Instead, she has focussed on her role as a working royal, something that this episode mentions only briefly. It's a shame that it uses this facet of the underexplored Anne's story as the fulcrum for jealousy between princesses. At least it's not a catfight.

We've barely glimpsed Anne's relationship with her husband, Mark Philips, but by the time of this episode, it's in trouble. But because we've barely seen the wife, let alone her husband, it's difficult to care. Once again, *The Crown* relegates Anne's story to filler, hinting only vaguely at storylines that might have been, including the queen's mention of Anne's protection officer, Peter Cross, who was removed from the Princess Royal's household due to rumours of a relationship with his charge that went beyond professional. Anne is distressed at the removal of her close confidante and whilst in real life she's never spoken about Cross or their relationship, that hasn't stopped the scriptwriters before. Cross actually sold his story to a redtop at the time, but this is the season of Charles and Diana, so we were never going to see behind the closed doors of Anne's home.

The one thing Princess Anne can be glad of is that she isn't Prince Edward, depicted here as an entitled brat who spouts poor little rich boy-isms until even his mother is sick of hearing him. Prince Andrew, meanwhile, arrives by helicopter to charm his mum from first to last. Rumour has it that he was her favourite child, at least until the story of his relationship with Jeffrey Epstein made the headlines, and this is the conclusion reached by Peter Morgan too. Elizabeth comes alive when she is with Andrew just as Philip comes alive with Anne, whom he acknowledges as his own favourite. Again, this chimes with insider gossip.

Though *The Crown* can't touch the Epstein scandal since the timeline can only be twisted so much before it breaks, there is a reference to it in this episode. As Andrew gleefully discusses a movie in which his then-girlfriend, Koo Stark, stars as a 17-year-old girl undergoing her sexual awakening, the monarch asks if that's even legal. Andrew responds with an arch, "Who cares?". Point taken.

Because this *is* the Charles and Diana season – or the first of two-and-a-half Charles and Diana seasons – we soon learn that things are not happy at Highgrove, despite Diana's pregnancy. This, as the world now knows, was true. The marriage of the Prince and Princess of Wales was always tumultuous, and the happy event didn't change that.

4.5 Fagan

The Crown

As unemployment soars, Mrs Thatcher tells the queen that the Falkland Islands have been recaptured. Michael Fagan, dissatisfied with his lack of employment at a time when a fortune is being spent on war, complains to his disinterested Member of Parliament, who facetiously suggests that he should tell his troubles to the queen. Fagan takes his comments to heart and decides to do just that.

Pushed to his limit when social services take his children from him, Fagan breaks into the palace and encounters the queen in her bedroom. Though he begs her to save the nation from Margaret Thatcher, Elizabeth can do little to prevent the jubilant PM from starring in her very own victory parade.

The Truth

This is one of those episodes in which *The Crown* takes the basic facts of a situation and embroiders them to create a narrative. That's never more clear than in Morgan's depiction of Michael Fagan, who is reimagined as a man pushed to his limits by the nation's economic situation. Whilst he was one of the millions unemployed and trapped in a seemingly hopeless situation and whilst he did indeed breach Buckingham Palace security on more than one occasion, that's where fact and fiction part company.

In *Fagan*, the titular character is motivated to break into Buckingham Palace by the dismissive attitude of his Conservative Member of Parliament. Both the meeting with the MP and the MP himself are fictional; Fagan's constituency was represented by the SDP and he had never met his Member of Parliament. The scenes in which Fagan shins over a fence to access palace grounds do resemble the reality of his escapades, as does the moment when he pours a glass of wine during his initial trespass. That first visit to the palace took place in the early days of July 1982 and Fagan shinned up a drainpipe, only to be spotted by a maid who raised the alarm, just as the episode depicts. However, when officers could find no trace of him, the report was discounted as an error. In fact, Fagan returned that same night to enjoy a snack of royal cheese and crackers. In *The Crown*, the intruder's actions are discussed with the queen and the Duke of Edinburgh by Martin Charteris, but Her Majesty declines to beef up security. Needless to say, this is scriptwriter's convenience on full display.

It is Fagan's second visit that really concerns Peter Morgan. In *The Crown*, Michael Fagan lets himself into the queen's bedroom and despite her understandable panic at awakening to be confronted by an intruder, she remains calm and the duo have a conversation about the state of the nation. Despairing at the impact of Thatcher's policies and attitudes, Fagan begs the queen to do something to check the prime minister's power.

This, needless to say, is not how it happened. Fagan scaled a wall and, as he crossed the grounds and entered the palace, was detected by an alarm. Unfortunately, police at the scene suspected a faulty wire and simply switched the alarm off without conducting any further investigations, leaving Fagan to enjoy an impromptu wander through Buckingham Palace. He eventually reached the queen's bedroom just after seven o'clock in the morning, having cut his hand on a broken glass ashtray. As the series shows, he managed to slip into the bedroom during the shift changeover for the officer who was guarding the monarch's door. It was a scenario that none had thought possible and that might have had dire consequences.

Though newspaper reports at the time did claim that Fagan had sat on the queen's bed and chatted to her, that wasn't the case, and there was certainly no veracity to the odd claims that the queen had worn a *Carry On*-style baby doll nightie. Instead, Fagan recalled that Her Majesty pressed an alarm button beside her bed, then summoned the help of a maid and a footman. The intruder was swiftly detained by police and the whole affair led to an overhaul of the palace security system, which had failed multiple times during Fagan's visits. Because trespass wasn't a criminal offence, Fagan faced no charges, but he was detained for psychiatric evaluation for three months. A charge of theft for drinking the royal wine was dropped, whilst trespassing on royal property did not become a criminal offence until 2007, a quarter of a century after Michael Fagan paid a visit to Queen Elizabeth II.

The events took place on 9 July 1982, more than a fortnight after the Argentinian surrender in the Falklands, but *Fagan* depicts the second break in as taking place the very next day. Dramatically this makes a certain sense, as the programme uses the incident as the driving force for a conversation between the queen and Mrs Thatcher in which we see their very different worldviews. Since the audiences between Elizabeth and her prime ministers were always confidential, we can't know what her true relationship with Mrs Thatcher was, but rumour has it that things could indeed be tense. However, whilst the fictional Thatcher is often depicted as being bullish or condescending in *The Crown*, the real Mrs T was an ardent royalist who remained in awe of the sovereign, no matter how many times they met. That reverence did nothing to smooth the formality of their regular audiences.

Fagan, however, depicts things differently. As a contemplative sovereign reflects on Michael Fagan's warnings about Thatcher, the prime minister heads off to headline a victory parade in front of a cheering crowd numbering tens of thousands of people. She leaves the wistful monarch alone in Buckingham Palace to watch helplessly as her prime minister takes the salute in her place. The narrative thrust is very clear: Mrs Thatcher has arrogantly supplanted the queen and taken her place at the heart of victory celebrations. That's not how it happened. Whilst the Falklands War ended on 14 June, weeks before the Fagan incident, the parade didn't take place until autumn, when Queen Elizabeth was out of the country on an official visit. Indeed, she had already taken centre stage herself at the thanksgiving service in St Paul's Cathedral that summer. That, of course, is absent from *Fagan*.

4.6 Terra Nullius

The Crown

In Australia, incoming Republican prime minister Bob Hawke is swept to office on a tide of republican fervour. As he prepares to welcome Charles and Diana to the country, he hopes that the outrageous cost of their tour will be the tipping point for a referendum.

The Prince and Princess of Wales are joined on their trip by the infant Prince William, much to Charles's annoyance. Things between the couple go from bad to worse as they argue about Camilla and Dimania sweeps Australia, leaving also-ran Charles piqued as he is elbowed out of the spotlight in favour of his dazzling wife. His bitter reaction to

Diana's popularity exacerbates her eating disorder and a short-lived reconciliation ends in misery.

Upon their return to England, Diana seeks comfort from the queen but an unsympathetic Elizabeth, jealous of the princess's popularity, shuns her embrace.

The Truth

When the Prince and Princess of Wales visited the Antipodes in 1983, Diana insisted on bucking accepted royal protocol and took her infant son Prince William along with her. This has since been heralded as one of the new princess's first modernising moments, as she refused to leave her baby at home whilst she carried out her duties. Just as *Terra Nullius* shows, Diana really did outshine Charles during the visit to Australia and New Zealand, but as ever there's a lot of massaging for drama going on.

Firstly, whilst Hawk was a Republican, to show him quite so rabid and foul-mouthed in opposition to the royal visit as *Terra Nullius* does requires a fair bit of dramatic license. There's a fair bit more in Diana's outburst when she claims that she doesn't know where William is staying and insists on completely rewriting the whole itinerary so she can be taken to him. The princess knew full well that William was being cared for by handpicked nurses at a sheep ranch in Woomargama, New South Wales, because she and Charles spent time there with him during the tour. There was no need for panicky changes to the schedule to suit the hysterical Princess of Wales either, because everything had already been planned to the nth degree specifically to avoid unforeseen catastrophe. It's odd that the queen seems to think she only visited Australia once and watches film of her 1954 tour with an air of nostalgic longing. Why she has forgotten that she made more than half a dozen additional trips down under trip is a mystery.

What is true is that Diana struggled during the tour. Jet lag, heat and the sheer size of the crowds who clamoured to get a look at her proved too much for the inexperienced princess and she broke down in tears outside Sydney Opera House, something that none of that clamouring crowd seemed to notice. *The Crown* plays heavily on Diana's struggles with the spotlight and her unsympathetic husband, making much of Charles's apparently dismissive arrogance when heat forced her to abandon an attempted hike up Uluru. Whilst Diana did decline to make the full ascent, it wasn't because of her health or emotional fragility, but for the far more prosaic reason that she feared flashing the world's press as she descended in a billowy skirt.

In fact, the world's press was already discussing the princess's apparent fragility and shyness and putting bets on how that would manifest. Whether Diana would cry, explode or soar, they were ready to capture every moment of it on camera, just as they would be for the rest of her life. The palace was waiting with bated breath to see how the Princess of Wales fared too and at first, things went badly. Sunburned and shattered, Diana seemed to be faltering as she admitted that the heat was proving an ordeal; Charles himself apologised to a sympathetic Australian media for their obvious jetlag, admitting that both he and his wife were struggling on the first days of the trip.

But Diana didn't sink; instead, much to everyone's surprise, she sparkled. And whilst his wife was undoubtedly the star of the show, Charles didn't fare too badly either. The couple were met with a rapturous reception wherever they went, but it was Diana who really charmed the crowds, coming across as a relatable young woman who was keen to talk about her experience as a new mum above all things. There wasn't a hint of stuffiness about her and she blossomed and shone whenever she discussed little William, winning the hearts of just about everyone who turned out to meet her. Unfortunately, this sparkling stardom did indeed get right on Charles's wick as Diana herself admitted during her bombshell 1995 *Panorama* interview. Her husband, she realised, was jealous of her popularity. It was something he was going to have to get used to.

And then there was the hug. The moment the monarch rejects her distressed daughter-in-law's embrace is full of meaning in *Terra Nullius*, capturing as it does not only the differences between the women, but the moment at which Diana's isolation within the royal family is made painfully complete. Though he wasn't an eyewitness to the moment, Prince Harry himself related the story of his mother attempting to embrace the queen, something that was absolutely forbidden. Her Majesty dodged the embrace and the whole thing ended with an awkward apology.

Whilst *The Crown* spends a lot of time examining the apparent disconnect between Diana and her mother-in-law, what it does less well is depict their relationship before things turned sour. Though the on-screen queen is initially delighted with Diana, by the time the couple return from their tour, things are stiff, awkward and cold. In reality, Diana and the monarch actually enjoyed a warm relationship, at least at the start, and the princess often sought Elizabeth's comfort as her marriage crumbled. Although their relationship did eventually decline, the queen didn't dismiss Diana cruelly as she does in the end of *Terra Nullius*; instead, she was receptive to the Princess of Wales's impromptu and highly emotional visits and was surprisingly adept at calming her daughter-in-law and comforting her distress. But where's the drama in that?

4.7 The Hereditary Principle

The Crown

As Prince Edward begins his life as a working royal, Princess Margaret finds that her own duties are to be reduced. Whilst recuperating from an operation to remove part of her lung, the troubled princess begins to consult a therapist and is horrified to learn that two cousins she had thought long-since dead, Nerissa and Katherine Bowes-Lyon, are actually in a mental institution.

When Margaret confronts her mother, the queen claims that the family had no choice, but Margaret is tormented by the fear that she too will succumb to madness.

The Truth

The Crown's depiction of Princess Margaret has never been the most sympathetic. She's either barking at someone or going mad and many of her most important biographical moments have been framed through the eyes or words of other characters. She has been largely silent in her own story at times when her point of view would have been very welcome indeed.

The Hereditary Principle gives Margaret a whole episode to herself, though it is to both tell someone else's story and to once again suggest that Margaret is not quite stable. As depicted in the episode, Princess

Margaret did undergo an operation to remove part of her lung in 1985, as a lifetime of heavy smoking began to take its toll on her health. However, she wasn't in treatment at the time of Prince Edward's 21st birthday celebrations, because he turned 21 10 months later. Likewise, when Charles tells his brother in *The Hereditary Principle* that Diana is pregnant again, he must be mistaken: Prince Harry was born in 1984. Of course, in *The Crown* universe, as we know, time has always been elastic.

There is a little bit more fact fiddling when it comes to Margaret learning that, now Edward has come of age, he will take her place as a Counsellor of State. Margaret is devastated and feels as though she is being put out to pasture, whereas in reality, the Councillors of State have always been appointed in strict order of precedence. Though Margaret was disappointed to lose a role she enjoyed, she would have known from the off that it would happen when Edward reached 21. Likewise, the suggestion in *The Hereditary Principle* that she was stripped of her duties precisely when she needed the distraction most is a fiction: Margaret continued as a senior royal.

Though the series doesn't explain it, there are six Counsellors of State, two of whom are called upon to serve if the monarch goes abroad or is too ill to carry out their duties. The Counsellors of State at the time of this episode were Prince Philip, the Queen Mother and then, in order of precedence, the next four people in the line of succession. These were Prince Charles, Princess Anne, Prince Andrew and Princess Margaret. Once Edward came of age, he knocked Margaret out of the running.

At the start of the episode, Margaret and her chum Derek "Dazzle" Jenkins dance in the palace to David Bowie and Margaret, who is falling for Dazzle, is devastated to learn that he is going to become a priest. In fact, the princess and Dazzle really were close friends until his death in 1995, though here she drops him like a hot rock after he suggests she might like to consider a spiritual remedy for her troubles, rather than an alcoholic one. Margaret's cruel rejection of Dazzle's friendship in this episode is a useful way to further drive home the point that the princess is becoming ever more lonely and disenchanted with her life. As with earlier depictions of Margaret, though, showing her as constantly on the edge of breakdown feels like some fairly weak characterisation.

But Princess Margaret being on the edge is the catalyst for the whole episode. As she languishes miserably in Mustique, Prince Charles makes a fictional visit to advise his aunt to see a fictional therapist and that, dear reader, is where she learns of the unhappy fate of Nerissa and Katherine, two cousins whom she had long believed dead. Though the episode takes some liberties, the story of the two sisters and their three cousins is heart-breaking.

Nerissa and Katherine were the daughters of the Queen Mother's brother, John Herbert Bowes-Lyon, and his wife, Lady Elizabeth Hepburn-Stuart-Forbes-Trefusis. Born in 1919 and 1926 respectively, the sisters inherited a learning disability from their mother's side of the family and were confined to Earlswood Hospital in 1941. Whilst *Burke's Peerage* recorded that they had died in 1940 and 1961 respectively, Nerissa actually lived until 1986 and Katherine until 2014. Throughout their lives, they received neither visits, communication, nor any financial help from members of the royal family, whilst only members of hospital staff attended their funerals. Nerissa's grave was left unmarked until the media uncovered the existence of the two sisters in the late 1980s, at which point the royal family's apparent indifference to the fate of the sisters came under scrutiny. It was discovered that three more cousins of Nerissa and Katherine were also living at Earlswood, having inherited a genetic disease that proved fatal to male members of the Hepburn-Stuart-Forbes-Trefusis line, and caused a learning disability in the female side of the family.

Filtered through the narrative of *The* Crown, Margaret's discovery can only mean one thing, namely that the heartless Windsors will do anything to protect their precious line. We see Princess Margaret make a fictional trip to Earlswood, where she waits outside whilst Dazzle goes in and learns the truth. She then confronts the Queen Mother with what she has learned, only to be told that the sisters and their cousins were locked away in order to prevent any whisper of mental illness in the royal line. Yet this doesn't make any sense. After all, the Queen Mother knew that the disability was hereditary on the Hepburn-Stuart-Forbes-Trefusis side of the family, not the Bowes-Lyon side. The suggestion that the action was prompted by the abdication and the fear that people might start to think the Duke of Windsor mad for walking away from the throne simply doesn't hold water. In fact, the three cousins who were also placed in Earlswood had no blood ties to the House of Windsor at all. Which means, of course, that Princess Margaret is right: her family really do have cold blood in their veins. And it's about to get a whole lot colder.

4.8 48:1

The Crown

The queen and Margaret Thatcher clash over the use of sanctions on apartheid-era South Africa. Her Majesty believes that sanctions should be enforced in order to fight racial segregation and violence, whilst the prime minister holds that the move would only hurt Britain's trade. As the only nation holding out against voting in favour of sanctions at the Commonwealth Heads of Government Meeting, the UK causes a deadlock that doesn't break until Thatcher's demands for extensive amendments to the agreement are met. However, no sooner has she signed than she gives a troublesome press briefing.

Back in England, meanwhile, someone has leaked to the press that the queen and the prime minister are at odds. When Thatcher challenges the monarch on the leak, the queen assures her that she remains apolitical. However, she also tells her press secretary, Michael Shea, not to refute rumours of a rift between the Palace and Downing Street, only to sacrifice Shea as the supposed source of the leak.

The Truth

In *48:1*, we once again find ourselves with one foot in truth and one in fiction. In 1985, the Commonwealth nations assembled in the Bahamas for the Commonwealth Heads of Government Meeting. On the agenda was the matter of sanctions against South Africa, a measure which all the attendees other than Margaret Thatcher were ready to approve: only the UK refused to sign the agreement. As the discussions went on, the *Today* newspaper carried a front-page story suggesting that relations between the queen and Mrs Thatcher had degraded almost to the point of no return.

Things went from bad to worse when the queen discussed her frustration at Thatcher's intransigence with her press secretary, Michael Shea, shortly before someone briefed *The Sunday Times* about friction between the palace and Downing Street. The result was a bombshell story in which the sovereign was quoted as being dismayed by Mrs Thatcher's lack of empathy and compassion. *48:1* suggests that the person who leaked the story was none other than Shea, acting under the subtle instruction of Queen Elizabeth herself. Once the story was out, someone had to be blamed so Morgan has the Palace throw Shea under the bus, demanding that he sacrifice himself and resign in order to save the queen's blushes.

The reality is a little more muddy, but Shea was certainly the prime suspect for the leak and the man who ultimately took the fall. Questions were asked on the floor of the House of Commons and with every finger pointing at him, he faced intense criticism and calls for his resignation. Eventually, the beleaguered press secretary admitted to having been the source of the story, but claimed that his involvement had been taken out of context and that he had been the victim of misrepresentation. Whether that is true or not, what is in little doubt is that Shea acted under his own steam, rather than the Machiavellian influence of the queen. In addition, though *The Crown* seems to suggest that Shea went immediately after the story broke, he actually moved on to a new job in 1987, as well as finding success in a second career as a prolific author of political thrillers.

As for the rift between Thatcher and the queen, nobody really knows. What is hugely unlikely, however, is that Margaret Thatcher would have dared to carpet the monarch during their audience as she does in this episode. Though Her Majesty is unbowed and retains her coolness, Thatcher keeps on pushing, challenging the queen in a manner that is as audacious as it is unbelievable. She simply wouldn't have dared. Of course, we will never have full facts on that relationship. The institution of the Crown has always remained staunchly apolitical in public and that wasn't about to change for the sake of Michael Shea or Peter Morgan.

4.9 Avalanche

The Crown

Charles and Diana are visiting the Royal Opera House to celebrate Charles's birthday. Diana has a special surprise in store for her husband and takes to the stage with dancer Wayne Sleep to perform a dance routine to Billy Joel's *Uptown Girl*, much to the prince's horror.

As trouble rumbles on, the couple take a skiing trip in Switzerland and narrowly escape an avalanche that kills their friend, Hugh Lindsay. Upon their return, the Prince and Princess of Wales are called to a meeting with the queen and the Duke of Edinburgh at which the Wales' mutual infidelity is the only topic of conversation. Diana promises that she will be faithful but Charles parents don't allow their son to speak. When he pours out his heart to Camilla, she tells him that they have to be realistic about their affair whilst Diana, despite her promises to the contrary, plunges back into her own affair with James Hewitt.

The Truth

There's not much point in confirming that *The Crown* is right to suggest that the marriage between the Prince and Princess of Wales was in crisis in the mid-1980s, as that's much picked over public knowledge by now. But in the interests of completeness, consider it noted.

In December 1985, the Friends of Covent Garden gave a private gala to celebrate the 37th birthday of Prince Charles. Much to everyone's surprise, during an unscheduled pause in the performance, dancer Wayne Sleep came out from the wings to the accompaniment of Billy Joel's hit, *Uptown Girl*. Moments later he was joined by the Princess of Wales for a dance duet that made headlines. Diana was sure that her husband would be overjoyed, but she had badly misjudged him. Charles, as *Avalanche* suggests, was mortified. It just wasn't his style.

The Prince of Wales is left to cringe with embarrassment all over again when he and his wife exchange anniversary gifts. His present to Diana is a nineteenth-century history of her family estate; Diana's offering to Charles is a videotape. He is horrified to find that it contains a video of the Princess of Wales in full costume and make-up as Christine, the leading lady of *The Phantom of the Opera*, Diana's favourite musical. Charles looks on in mute disbelief as his wife drifts around the West End set of Andrew Lloyd Webber's megahit, regaling him with a rendition of *All I Ask of You*, one of the show's big romantic numbers. Wow.

Whilst you could be forgiven for assuming that this scene was invented by the scriptwriters, Diana did give her husband a video cassette for the anniversary, but nobody knows exactly what was on it. She certainly visited the Phantom's London home at the Prince of Wales Theatre before the anniversary, where she had a whole afternoon with composer Lloyd Webber in which he put the sets and costumes at her disposal, but he has never spoken of what Diana got up to during her visit. The most likely explanation is that Diana, a talented dancer, filmed a dance performance on the stage rather than sang a song, but the tape has quite understandably never been made public. In *The Crown*, however, the princess's unwanted gift of a music video perfectly skewers the deep and enduring differences between husband and wife.

More than two years later, which translates to the very next day in *The Crown*'s timeline, the beleaguered couple went to Klosters in Switzerland to enjoy a skiing holiday. During their trip, an avalanche struck that killed Major Hugh Lindsay, an equerry to the queen who was also a good friend of Prince Charles. At the time of Lindsay's death, his pregnant wife, Sarah, worked in the royal press office, as depicted in the episode. Whilst Diana was back at the chalet with the pregnant Duchess of York when the avalanche hit, Charles was out skiing. When no word was received from the prince's party, fears began to mount that he might have been killed, fears that are reflected in the scenes set back in England, where the royals are anxiously awaiting news of his fate. Incidentally, the mention of Menai Bridge as a codename for the death of the Prince of Wales is accurate. Of course, the queen would already know what the codename was, but helpfully Martin Charteris is on hand to explain it to her anyway. Even though he had retired years earlier in favour of Philip Moore.

When the troubled Waleses are called in for a crisis meeting with Elizabeth and Philip, the prince is forbidden from speaking, whilst Diana promises to end her relationship with James Hewitt. Shortly afterwards she learns that Charles and Camilla are still seeing one another, so resumes her own affair. Diana met Major James Hewitt, an officer in the Household Cavalry, when he was asked to give her riding lessons. What began as a platonic relationship developed into a full-blown affair in 1986, which eventually lasted until 1991.

Because so much of this episode revolves around the discussion of the Wales' marriage, it's difficult to know for sure what is truth and what is fiction, but in broad strokes there is a lot that is accurate here. The avalanche struck Klosters on 10 March 1988, two years after Diana began her affair with Hewitt and Charles resumed his with Camilla. The timeline is massaged as ever, but the basic facts are in place and the stage is set for scandal as Charles sends shadowy men to watch his wife's liaisons with her lover and report back to him. The main takeaway from *Avalanche* is that things in the House of Windsor are Not Good. And so it will continue.

4.10 War

The Crown

It's the end of an era as Margaret Thatcher's leadership is challenged in Parliament by her deputy, Geoffrey Howe. Fearing that she may be about to lose her grip on office, Thatcher asks the queen to dissolve Parliament and thereby save her bacon, but Her Majesty refuses. After losing a bitter battle for survival, Mrs Thatcher leaves Downing Street, comforted only by the queen's gift of the prestigious Order of Merit.

With Diana and Hewitt very much back on, the princess travels to New York and wows the Big Apple, leading to an earthquake of a confrontation with her husband upon her return. Charles wants Camilla, but Camilla is terrified of facing the public if their affair is revealed. A furious Charles clashes with the queen, who tells him there can be no divorce. Diana, hoping to find a friend in the usually supportive Prince Philip, hears a few home truth from her father-in-law: *The Crown* must remain untarnished and the marriage cannot fail.

The Truth

"Like being savaged by a dead sheep" is how Dennis Healey memorably described his own clashes with Geoffrey Howe, yet it was the famously mild-mannered Howe who lit the fuse that would bring down Margaret Thatcher. Howe's resignation from the Cabinet in 1990 was the first move in a political powerplay that would end in Thatcher's resignation and the succession of John Major, just in time for season five.

What isn't true is that Thatcher tried to save her own skin by racing to the palace to beg the queen to dissolve Parliament, but in *War* it's suggested that a prompt dissolution would have brought her the time she needed to turn the tide and stay in power. Mrs Thatcher's biographers, both those who are in her corner and those who aren't, are agreed that this just wasn't Thatcher's style She didn't try to dodge the leadership contest, though she did fight tooth and nail to win it. Unlike Anthony Eden and Harold Macmillan in earlier seasons, this was a Tory prime minister who was determined to cling on with the tips of her fingers, regardless of what opponents and the electorate might want.

In the event, Margaret Thatcher could not achieve the victory she craved and, faced by the prospect of defeat by her own party colleagues, she chose to step down. Bitterly resentful towards the senior Tories she believed had betrayed her, she resigned on 28 November 1990; as *War* shows, the Iron Lady left Downing Street in tears.

As depicted in *The Crown*, the queen did give Thatcher the prestigious Order of Merit, a sure sign of the monarch's regard for the departing PM, regardless of the rumoured differences between them. At this point, it should be noted that, in a series that has often short-changed its female characters, the relationship between the monarch and this most divisive of her prime ministers is a prime example of a missed opportunity. In constantly presenting their meetings as some kind of simmering girl-against-girl feud, *The Crown* really shirked the opportunity to examine the real relationship between the monarch and the country's first female prime minister. It was complex and not always friendly, but nor was it the cold war of attrition presented here.

And so to the Waleses. Diana's trip to New York really was the triumph that we see on-screen and as has been well-documented, her compassion for and interest in the welfare of HIV AIDS patients at a time when the disease was stigmatised was ground-breaking. She did much to bring the disease into the public consciousness and most important of all, by hugging the patients she met and treating them just as she would anyone else, the princess sent a very clear message about groundless fears many had of contracting the disease. It was a cause that remained dear to her for the rest of her life.

What is notable by its absence, however, is any focus on Prince Charles's own charitable works. We see virtually nothing of his interest in the environment and conservation, nor of a passion for the natural world that was routinely mocked and held up for ridicule in the 1980s. Ironically, it's since been acknowledged that in many of these ecological interests, the embattled prince was ahead of his time. But Charles is this season's black-hearted villain; there are moments of empathy for him, but he's essentially a thoroughly bad lot, too busy making his wife miserable, being aloof with his children and obsessing over Camilla to be nice. And just as Camilla says, it's not the first time one of her family has intrigued with a Prince of Wales: her great-grandmother, Alice Keppel, enjoyed a long relationship with Edward, Prince of Wales. Though Edward was more than 25 years her senior, the relationship survived his succession to the throne as King Edward VII and ended only with his death.

Whilst it's accurate that Philip and Diana enjoyed a warm relationship, thinly veiled hints that the Duke of Edinburgh might be threatening his daughter-in-law are a little too on the nose. But *The Crown* is a big, glitzy soap opera and in that spirit, such scenes are very much in keeping with its ethos. So, as season four hurtles to a finish and we prepare for a whole new cast, it looks as though it's curtains for the Prince and Princess of Wales.

Yet despite what *War* suggests, during this period Prince Charles wasn't dreaming of a future with Camilla and he certainly wasn't angling for a divorce. At this stage, both he and Diana, as well as the queen and Prince Philip, hoped that the marriage might still be saved. It would only be a couple of years before all had to admit that there would be no happy ending for the Prince and Princess of Wales, but things had not quite reached the point of no return. Yet.

Seasons 5 and 6

Notable Cast

Queen Elizabeth II	Imelda Staunton
Prince Philip, Duke of Edinburgh	Jonathan Pryce
Dodi Fayed	Khalid Abdalla
Kate Middleton	Meg Bellamy
Mohamed Al-Fayed	Salim Daw
Tony Blair	Bertie Carvel
Peter Townsend	Timothy Dalton
Diana, Princess of Wales	Elizabeth Debicki
Prince Harry	Fflyn Edwards/Luther Ford
Anne, Princess Royal	Claudia Harrison
Prince William	Rufus Kampa/Ed McVey
Penny Knatchbull	Natascha McElhone
Princess Margaret	Lesley Manville
John Major	Jonny Lee Miller
Martin Bashir	Prasanna Puwanarajah
Hasnat Khan	Humayun Saeed
Andrew Morton	Andrew Steele
Queen Elizabeth The Queen Mother	Marcia Warren
Charles, Prince of Wales	Dominic West
Camilla Parker Bowles	Olivia Williams

SEASON 5

5.1 Queen Victoria Syndrome

The Crown

In 1991, Prince Charles is briefly basking in some excellent press that suggests the majority of the public would support him as monarch, should his mother abdicate. His balloon promptly bursts when he realises that his popularity is due in large part to the fact that he is married to Princess Diana. The Prince and Princess of Wales go on a second honeymoon despite wanting very different things out of it: Charles dreams of antiquity, Diana of sandy beaches and clear oceans. Charles abandons the trip, blaming a diary conflict as he dashes home to see Camilla.

When prime minister John Major visits Balmoral amid mounting tensions, he is thrown by a request that the country should pay to renovate the royal yacht Britannia, something he is fundamentally opposed to. After listening to each of the senior royals spill out their problems to him in turn, Major tells his wife Norma that the family is in such turmoil that their private miseries might well spill out into the public arena.

The Truth

It's eyes down for season five and be warned, this is very much the Charles and Diana show – even more so than season four. In fact, there's very little else going on in this batch of ten episodes beyond the slow and agonising breakdown of the turbulent Wales' marriage. What respite there is comes with a hefty dollop of symbolism, just to plug the gaps between separation and divorce.

116

Queen Victoria Syndrome starts as it means to go on, as a young queen launches the Royal Yacht Britannia, drawing parallels in her speech between the new vessel's first voyage and her own tentative steps as sovereign. It's no surprise to learn that the episode continues that parallel, as we see the old yacht way past its prime and in danger of being decommissioned, just as the queen is starting to feel every one of her 65 years. Elizabeth's advancing years will be a common theme in this season, as the next generation takes centre stage in the full glare of the world's media.

The Sunday Times opinion poll, in which the majority of respondents state that the queen should abdicate in favour of her eldest son, is a fictional amalgamation of several such polls. Peter Morgan has mixed them all together to suggest that the queen was increasingly seen to be out of touch, whilst Prince Charles's own popularity relied in a large part on that of Diana, the public's avowed darling. This was true: by 1991, Dimania was an unstoppable phenomenon. With Andrew Morton's bombshell book *Diana: Her True Story,* on the horizon, you can already guess what we're in for.

The Prince and Princess of Wales did indeed take their family on a cruise around the Med, in what was widely touted as a second honeymoon to mark their 10th anniversary. They were joined by King Constantine and Queen Anne-Marie of Greece, alongside Charles's cousin Lord Romsey and his wife and children. Penelope Knatchbull, Lady Romsey, was to become a fast friend of Prince Philip, Duke of Edinburgh, and this is the first glimpse viewers get of her prior to her becoming a featured character in later episodes. Penny is the wife of Norton Knatchbull, Prince Philip's godson and grandson of the late Lord Mountbatten.

One thing we know about *The Crown* is that it never flinches from tapping even the most questionable sources of drama; in this episode, however, flinch is exactly what it does. In reality, the Knatchbulls' young daughter, Leonora fell ill whilst on a trip to Majorca with the Waleses in 1990 and had to be rushed for emergency medical treatment. Only then did her parents learn that she was suffering from kidney cancer. Photographs of Charles comforting Penny in the immediate aftermath of the diagnosis were published by tabloid newspapers under headlines that suggested there was scandal afoot; those headlines drew the ire of Norton Knatchbull and resulted in an apology from *The Sun. Queen*

Victoria Syndrome, however, resists dramatising any of this and instead features the cruise that the two families took in 1991 instead, when all present believed that Leonora was in remission. Sadly, her recovery was temporary and the little girl lost her battle in October 1991, when she was just five years old. During her final weeks in hospital, the Princess of Wales was a regular visitor to Leonora's bedside.

Contrary to *The Crown*'s suggestion, Princess Diana was not Leonora's godmother, but godmother to her older sister, Alexandra. In addition, Charles didn't really flee the cruise for a rendezvous with Camilla; instead, immediately before his second honeymoon, he enjoyed a painting retreat in Tuscany. Supposedly quite by coincidence, Camilla just happened to be take a break of her own, a mere half an hour from Charles's villa.

Elsewhere, *Queen Victoria Syndrome* takes a brisk gallop through a pick and mix of other royal issues with mixed regard for the facts. The Royal Yacht Britannia was very much in need of renovation at the taxpayer's expense and it's safe to assume that Princess Anne did indeed find equerry Timothy Laurence attractive, since she eventually married him. However, she was already in a relationship with Laurence by 1989, two years before she catches her first glimpse of him in *The Crown*. And once again Anne is given the shortest of short change, still married in episode one but divorced and ready to mingle by episode four. This, as per *The Crown*'s habitual approach to Princess Anne's story, is something that happens largely off screen. Beyond that, as far the House of Windsor is concerned, there's a whole lot of fiction. There's never been any suggestion that Charles was champing at the bit for his mother to abdicate and, since there was no such *Sunday Times* poll, members of the royal household had no need to try and hide the paper from the queen. Such is drama.

And then we come to the prime minister. Sir John Major has been vocal in his criticism of the series and its depiction of his relationship with the queen. He has gone on record to state that the scenes showing his heart to hearts with members of the family never happened and that the mildly critical, though very sympathetic, views of royalty espoused by him on-screen are likewise fictional. At least he does speak though: like so many other political wives, Norma has very little to say.

It's likely obvious to viewers that scenes in which the queen rhapsodises lyrically about Britannia are straight out of a scriptwriter's brain but, as we know, audiences between the monarch and the prime minister are confidential. The truth is that whilst we will never know exactly what was said, we can hazard a guess that the queen wouldn't have been quite so flowery when discussing renovations to her yacht. That being said, when the estimate for repairs to the vessel came in at a cool £20 million, John Major's government decided that it was simply too expensive to give the refurbishment the greenlight. It was the beginning of the end for Britannia.

5.2 The System

The Crown

When Leonora Knatchbull's death plunges her family into mourning. Prince Philip reaches out to her bereaved mother, Penny, to offer his support. For Charles and Diana, things are about to step up a gear as Diana's friend, radiologist James Colthurst, informs the princess that a journalist named Andrew Morton intends to tell her story in a no-holds-barred biography, Diana agrees to cooperate on the condition that her involvement is kept a secret and that she has no direct contact with Morton. Instead, Colthurst will deliver his questions and record her answers on tape.

As Philip grows closer to Penny over a shared love for carriage driving, she tells him that there are rumours regarding Diana and Morton. As the book progresses, things take a sinister turn when Colthurst is involved in a car accident and Morton's home is ransacked, before the once supportive Philip gives Diana a chilling warning on the eve of the publication of *Diana: Her True Story*.

The Truth

Sadly, the events that *The Crown* depicts around the death of Leonora Knatchbull are more or less accurate. Leonora, the granddaughter of Earl Mountbatten, passed away in October 1991, aged just five years old. She was laid to rest at the Mountbatten family's Broadlands estate; three years after her death, the Leonora Children's Cancer Fund was established in her memory.

The Duke of Edinburgh and Penny Knatchbull, later Countess Mountbatten of Burma, really did enjoy a long and enduring friendship that was forged in the aftermath of the tragedy. Penny was married to Philip's godson, Norton Knatchbull, and their close friendship has certainly attracted one or two undeserved raised eyebrows over the years. Whilst it's true that the Duke of Edinburgh took up carriage driving after he retired from playing polo and offered to teach Penny the ropes, the story of the refurbished coach that features in this episode appears to be fictitious.

The unlikely friendship between the couple endured to the end of Philip's life and Penny became a close friend to many of the Windsors. She was a regular attendee at royal events and if further evidence was needed of the friendship, Prince Charles actually gave away her daughter Alexandrea on her wedding day. Whilst *The Crown* is careful not to even hint at anything untoward between the friends, it can't resist suggesting that the queen was jealous of her husband's younger female friend. Again, this seems more like a scriptwriter's invention than the reality.

Away from the Duke of Edinburgh, Princess Diana is stuck in an ever-twisting elastic timeframe as she arrives at St Thomas's Hospital to perform the opening of a new scanner unit in 1991. In reality, it was five years earlier. This serves to introduce us to her friend, Doctor James Colthurst, and offers viewers a quick glimpse of the now infamous journalist Andrew Morton, who is skulking about with an ingratiating smile before inveigling himself with Colthurst. What we see of the writing of *Diana: Her True Story*, though dramatic, is actually very close to the facts; sometimes, reality doesn't need any embroidering. A note on the timeline though: by the time Diana and Charles went on the trip we see in episode one, it's very likely that the princess was already secretly working on the book with Morton.

James Colthurst and Princess Diana had been friends since they met during a skiing holiday when Diana was 17 years old. They moved in the same social circles so, when Diana twisted her ankle, medical student Colthurst was drafted in to examine her injury. It was the start of a lifelong friendship. Though Diana didn't open the new unit in 1991, but 1986, it was at this event that Colthurst first met journalist Andrew Morton. Their friendship developed and over squash games in the hospital, as depicted in *The System*, Morton confided in Colthurst that he was writing a biography of the princess.

As *The Crown* asserts, it was Colthurst who first told Diana of the book and it was he who served as the middleman. Once the princess gave her consent to collaborate anonymously on the project, Colthurst would meet Diana at Kensington Palace with Morton's questions and a tape recorder hidden in a briefcase, in order to smuggle it past Diana's aides and palace officials. Colthurst then recorded Diana's answers on cassettes which he delivered to the journalist. The princess was fully aware of the subterfuge, of course.

Just as in season four, this is very much the Diana version of events, so don't expect to see or hear much about the princess's own indiscretions. The series also elects not to choose a side when it comes to Diana's suspicions that her telephone was bring bugged. As work progressed on the book she became increasingly convinced that sinister forces were conspiring against her, fears that grew with each passing day. Whilst we see the princess listening with concern to odd clicking noises on her telephone line, neither we nor Diana ever learn conclusively if she was really being bugged.

As things gather pace, Colthurst is knocked off his bike and Morton's home is ransacked. These two events did more or less happen as dramatised, with the slight caveat that the break-in was actually at Morton's office, rather than his home. Once *Diana: Her True Story* hit the shelves, it became a phenomenon. It blew the lid off the unhappy Wales' marriage and left the world's media speculating about whether the princess herself was the person who'd spilled the beans. Morton was asked constantly if Diana had been one of his anonymous sources, but he stuck to their agreement and told everyone who asked that the princess had no involvement whatsoever in the work. After Diana's death, however, he finally confirmed that she had collaborated on the book.

Things depart from reality when Penny warns Philip that she has heard rumours about the book. This couldn't have happened, simply because nobody beyond Colthurst had the slightest idea that Diana and Morton were engaged in their clandestine project. Given the conspiracy theories that swirled and continue to swirl today regarding Diana's death, to suggest that a malevolent Prince Philip made veiled threats to his daughter-in-law can only be a conscious creative decision, aimed at whipping up foreboding given that we know what the future holds. In truth, the Duke of Edinburgh couldn't have made sinister threats to Diana before the book was released, because neither he nor the Knatchbulls knew anything of its existence, so secretive was the project. The Duke of Edinburgh finally got the full picture a year after publication, when he settled down for an overnight flight with a copy of *Diana: Her True Story* for company.

Far from reacting with cold fury to the biography, once Philip knew of the book's contents, he actually opened a dialogue with Diana by letter. Though this was far from an easy ride, the duke's exchanges with his beleaguered daughter-in-law were warm, honest and even sympathetic. In this correspondence, he accepted Diana's claims that she was not involved in *Diana: Her True Story* and focused instead on how the marriage of the prince and princess might be saved. That, of course, was not to be.

5.3 Mou Mou

The Crown

Egypt, 1946, and Coca-Cola street seller Mohamed Fayed – he had yet to add the "Al" - has a fleeting experience with the Duke and Duchess of Windsor, aka Edward and Mrs Simpson. More than thirty years later, Al-Fayed is now the millionaire owner of the Hôtel Ritz Paris, where he forces his reluctant son, Dodi, to fire a black waiter named Sydney Johnson. However, once he learns that Johnson was previously valet to the Duke of Windsor, Al-Fayed appoints him to his personal staff. Johnson becomes an invaluable guide as Al-Fayed navigates the minefield of the British upper classes, teaching him proper etiquette and protocol as he branches out into the UK as the owner of Harrods.

When the Duchess of Windsor dies in 1986, Al-Fayed leases the late Duke and Duchess's villa in Paris and invites Her Majesty the Queen to visit. Instead, she sends her secretary, Sir Robert Fellowes, who has a list of items he is to seize for the Royal Collection. As Al-Fayed nurses Sydney Johnson on his death bed, he reflects on his treatment at the hands of the royal family, little knowing that he will soon be rejected by the queen again.

Elizabeth dodges Al-Fayed's efforts to meet him at the Royal Windsor Horse Show and instead sends Diana. In reality, Diana had met Dodi at a polo match in 1986, but here Al-Fayed briefly introduces his son to the princess. As their afternoon together continues, Mohamed Al-Fayed and Princess Diana find that they have more in common than they might ever have guessed and against the odds, the two outsiders hit it off.

The Truth

First things first: the Duke and Duchess of Windsor didn't visit Egypt in 1946 and didn't enchant Mohamed Al-Fayed. Since the conceit of this episode is that he was somehow inspired throughout life by having seen the couple once through the railings of their expensive country club, such a fiction was, we assume, necessary. Also make believe are the scenes in which Al-Fayed fires Sydney Johnson because of his ethnicity, only to rehire him due to his Windsor connection and subsequently nurse him on his deathbed. It's a curious retelling of Al-Fayed's life and one that is, as we've seen so many times, a cocktail of truth and fiction.

Sydney Johnson, who we have glimpsed in earlier episodes around the Duke and Duchess of Windsor's orbit, was a Bahaman who began working as a footman for the couple when he was 16, during the duke's tenure as Governor of the Bahamas. When the Windsors moved to Paris he came with them, by now promoted to valet, and remained in their service for over three decades. So close was he to the duke that he was one of the very select group of retainers invited to attend his late employer's funeral. Johnson left his employment with the Duchess of Windsor in 1973, the year after the death of the duke, though whether he resigned or was sacked depends on whose account you believe.

Eventually, Sydney Johnson took a job as a waiter at the Hôtel Ritz Paris. It was here that he met Mohamed Al-Fayed in 1979, soon after the Egyptian had become owner of the Ritz in a £20 million deal. Al-Fayed, who nursed ambitions to enter British high society, was drawn to Johnson due to both his past employment history and his extensive understanding and insider knowledge of the world that the businessman was so desperate to join. This was why he engaged Johnson as his personal valet, not because he had an obsessive fascination with the Duke and Duchess of Windsor, as *Mou Mou* would have us believe. Though it's highly unlikely that Johnson was some sort of Henry Higgins to his new employer, he did encourage him to lease the villa after the death of the Duchess of Windsor, shoring up Al-Fayed's belief that in doing so, he would win the favour of the royal family. Johnson became a trusted retainer in the Al-Fayed household, remaining in his service until his death in 1990.

But for all Sydney Johnson has his part to play in this episode, it is very much the Al-Fayed story that Morgan wants to tell. And, to a large degree, he does so faithfully. Whilst selling Coca-Cola on the streets of Alexandria, Al-Fayed's drive and ambition caught the eye of the mega-rich businessman, Adnan Khashoggi, with whom he began a successful and lucrative professional relationship. That relationship became personal in 1954, when Al-Fayed married Khashoggi's sister, Samira. Though the marriage lasted just two years, the couple became parents to Dodi during this time.

The Crown goes out of its way to depict Al-Fayed as an outsider during his rise through the social ranks, with his multi-million pound purchase of The Ritz Paris subject to suspicion and scrutiny from the snobbish officials overseeing the sale. As he makes the deal, at his side is his faithful lieutenant, Dodi. This is definitely a bit of dramatic license, as is the scene in which he has Dodi fire Sydney Johnson due to his race; what these scenes do, of course, is make it clear that Dodi would do anything to win the love and respect of his father. As Al-Fayed completes his purchase of Harrods, one thing is constantly pushed to the forefront: he desperately wants to be part of the British establishment and more than anything, he wants his British passport. As history has since told, despite becoming the owner of Harrods, he never got it.

Mou Mou hints that Al-Fayed was never quite able to secure the meeting with the queen that he so longed for, but they actually met on more than one occasion. This episode depicts Her Majesty dodging Al-Fayed at the Harrods-sponsored Windsor Horse Show, whereas in reality it was at this event that he was photographed shaking hands with the monarch. Photographers captured the moment in images that left Al-Fayed delirious with happiness, but no closer to obtaining the elusive passport he desired.

Though much of the history of Al-Fayed shown in *Mou Mou* is true, there are some elements that are not. For instance, Sir Robert Fellowes never visited the former villa of the Duke and Duchess of Windsor to seize personal items for the Royal Collection on the insistence of Elizabeth II. Quite apart from anything else, he didn't become Private Secretary until nine months after Johnson's death in January 1990. In fact, Al-Fayed did offer the queen the late duke's personal effects but she politely and unsurprisingly turned him down, much to his chagrin. After he had spent over £12 million having the Villa Windsor restored, hoping that it would ingratiate him into the royal favour, Al-Fayed singularly failed to understand that the grand gesture was as unwelcome as it was unnecessary: the family had no desire to honour the memory of their troublesome uncle.

What this episode does successfully capture in its fictionalised way is the friendship that developed between the businessman and the Princess of Wales, even though it doesn't focus too much on his existing ties to the Spencer family. Indeed, Al-Fayed was close friends with Diana's father and stepmother, who was a member of the Harrod's board. Thanks to this connection to Earl and Countess Spencer, whenever Diana visited Harrods, he made sure that she received his personal attention. Though Al-Fayed certainly enjoyed being in the spotlight, those who knew him suggest that his sympathy and affection for the princess was real. His critics, needless to say, have a different opinion.

One final thing to note is the presence of a tantalising collection of personal diaries written by the Duke of Windsor, which Fellowes spirits away, never to be seen again. Alas, there's no evidence that the late duke kept a personal diary that was seized by representatives of the Crown, explosive though it might have been.

5.4 Annus Horribilis

The Crown

In 1992, years after they were torn apart, Peter Townsend writes to Princess Margaret to inform her that he is coming to London to attend a reception for veterans. When the couple are reunited for the first time in nearly four decades, Townsend tells Margaret that he wishes to return her love letters. The former lovers rekindle their friendship and share a goodbye kiss in the gardens of Kensington Palace.

As a heartbroken Margaret comes to terms with the fact that the man she has always loved is terminally ill, newly divorced Princess

Anne is keen to marry Commander Timothy Laurence. It's the end of the road for Prince Andrew and Sarah Ferguson, though, as tabloids publish pictures of the Duchess of York having her toes sucked by an enthusiastic admirer. Just when it seems that things can't get any worse, a devastating fire rages through Windsor Castle.

The Truth

We already know that the circumstances of Princess Margaret's split from Peter Townsend weren't as they were depicted in *The Crown*, so take that as a given as we embark on our consideration of *Annus Horribliis*.

To kick off, the scenes showing Princess Margaret listening to her own episode of *Desert Island Discs* and becoming misty eyed to the strains of Hoagy Carmichael are a big dollop of romantic license. The princess appeared on *Desert Island Discs* in 1981, but she selected neither Hoagy Carmichael nor anything else that one might interpret as a veiled reference to her broken heart.

There's nothing *The Crown* loves more than a parallel plot and in this episode we finally get to see something of Princess Anne, who comes seeking the queen's blessing to marry Timothy Laurence. Just as Princess Margaret didn't get the permission she sought decades earlier, this time Elizabeth denies Anne the blessing she seeks. Unlike her aunt Margaret, however, Anne refuses to be cowed. She's done her duty to the Crown, she tells her mother, and she *will* marry Tim. Good on her.

Princess Anne married Mark Phillips in 1973 and the couple became parents to two children before their 1989 separation. By this time Anne had already met Laurence, who had been serving as an equerry to the queen for three years, and as the princess and her estranged husband moved on with their lives, she pursued her relationship with Laurence in earnest. The divorce of Princess Anne and Mark Philips was finalised in 1992; in December of that year, she married Timothy Laurence. The wedding had to take place in Scotland, since the Church of England at the time wouldn't permit divorced people to remarry in church if their first spouse was still alive. In Scotland, however, such a marriage was possible under specific circumstances. That marriage was a resounding success, though we will see next to nothing of it in *The Crown*.

And whilst we're on the subject of marriages, let's deal with the toe-sucking. Always a darling of the tabloid press, the Duchess of York and her husband, Prince Andrew, were separated in the early months of 1992, having already spent months apart. Headlines immediately began appearing that linked Sarah with a pick and mix of eligible men, among them an American named John Bryan. In 1992, the *Daily Mirror* published pictures of Bryan sucking the topless duchess's toes as she lounged beside a swimming pool, in what became one of the most enduring and inflammatory images of royal excess that modern audiences had ever seen. Whilst *Annus Horribilis* suggests that it was this photograph that finally prompted the Yorks to separate once and for all, they were already officially living apart by the time the images hit the newsstand. The Duke and Duchess of York were divorced in 1996, though the couple remain exceptionally close.

With Anne divorced and Andrew's marriage crumbling, it is up to Prince Charles to complete the hattrick of nuptial disaster when he drops by to tell his mother that he wants to be free of Diana once and for all. In *Annus Horribilis* he is set on divorce, but in truth he was still just about trying to keep the marriage alive, if only to spare his family the embarrassment of divorce. Just as *The Crown* suggests, there really was a huge amount of debate and gossip as three royal marriages fell like dominoes in the full glare of the public eye. It was the most turbulent time the House of Windsor had faced in years, but there was far worse to come.

And what of Margaret and Townsend, the one that got away? Their poignant reunion in *Annus Horribilis* puts a heart wrenching full stop on their relationship, but as always the reality was a little different. Though they had both been at a service for Her Majesty's 60th birthday at Windsor, the former lovers didn't come face to face until 1992. Having been invited to the same reception, Princess Margaret invited Peter Townsend and his wife to join her and other guests for lunch at Kensington Palace. Though Mrs Townsend tactfully declined, her husband attended and there, as though they had met only yesterday, the couple whiled away long hours chatting and reliving old times. After a walk in the gardens, they parted as friends; Townsend did not, however, bring with him the letters Margaret had written to him. These were never returned.

It was to be the last meeting between the princess and the Group Captain. Peter Townsend died of stomach cancer in 1995 and though Margaret didn't attend his funeral, the queen did send a letter of condolence to the man who had meant so much to her younger sister.

As royal marriages failed, 1992 still had one last unwanted card to play. The final disaster came at 11.15am on 20 November 1992, when a fire broke out in the Queen's Private Chapel at Windsor Castle, where a spotlight had caused a curtain to ignite. As the devastating blaze spread, the fire brigade battled the inferno desperately for over twelve hours, using 1.5 million gallons of water to douse the flames. When the cost was counted, it was revealed that the value of the items in the Royal Collection and the castle itself made them too valuable to insure: someone else would have to foot the bill. After much negotiation it was agreed that the repair bill would be settled by £2 million from the Queen, shored up by donations made to a restoration trust, and the proceeds of a new entry fee for visitors to Windsor Castle and Buckingham Palace. In return, for the first time in six decades, the British monarch would once again pay income tax.

Just as *Annus Horribilis* depicts, it was a rueful Queen Elizabeth II who gave a speech in honour of her Ruby Jubilee on 24 November. In it she described the challenging year as her "annus horribilis", an expression that has gone down in royal history.

5.5 The Way Ahead

The Crown

In 1992, Charles and Diana finally separate, with public opinion of the House of Windsor plummeting as the royal family try and fail to improve their popularity. Things only go from bad to worse when tabloids publish the transcript of an intimate telephone call between the Prince of Wales and Camilla Parker Bowles, which was secretly recorded by a radio ham three years earlier.

Desperate to regain ground, Charles takes part in an access-all-areas television documentary about his life, only to be knocked out of the headlines by Princess Diana, who attends an event in her infamous "revenge dress".

The Truth

Yes, it's the tampon episode. We all knew it was coming, and here it is: Camillagate. But before we discuss *that* telephone call, let's get the Way Ahead Group out of the way.

The Way Ahead Group was established by senior members of the royal family and their advisors to discuss what could be done to stay relevant in the modern era. Whilst *The Crown* depicts the group as woefully out of touch, the real royals all understood very well what was at stake, especially with multiple divorces happening seemingly all at once and acres of newsprint laying bare all their misfortunes to a ravenous public. Whilst Prince Charles does get a little bit of credit from scriptwriters for attempting to force modernisation against his mother's resistance, suggestions that he tried to establish a rival royal court are given a weight in *The Way Ahead* that they don't deserve. Charles did indeed set up his own court at St James's, but it wasn't intended to oppose his mother. Instead, the Prince of Wales's court was a place where he could further his own philanthropic interests and other projects; imagine it as a working group or subsidiary of sorts. It certainly wasn't anything sinister.

Having depicted Princess Diana's charitable interests, *The Way Ahead* finally shines a light, though not a very bright one, on Charles's work with the Prince's Trust. Unfortunately, one can't help but feel that this cursory trot through the Trust's projects is intended merely to cushion the inevitable complaints about what else *The Way Ahead* covers; Charles definitely doesn't have it easy from Peter Morgan.

In December 1992, just as *The Crown* shows, John Major announced the legal separation of the Prince and Princess of Wales to the House of Commons and the world. It was the formal confirmation of what had long been whispered: the fairytale marriage was on the rocks. A little while after the announcement was made, what has become known as Camillagate erupted when the *Daily Mirror* published a transcript of an intimate conversation between Charles and Camilla. According to the newspaper, the telephone call had been intercepted accidentally by a radio ham in Merseyside who was testing out a new piece of kit. As soon as he recognised the prince's voice coming through the airwaves, he hit the record button and captured the remainder of the call. Curiously, rather than immediately get on the blower to the nearest tabloid, he decided to keep the tape private for years before eventually selling it to the press. What is more intriguing in *The Way Ahead* is what isn't included; *The Crown* is definitely telling the Diana version of events.

What the episode doesn't cover is so-called Squidgygate, a 1992 scandal that involved Princess Diana and her own intercepted telephone call. In January 1990, a radio ham named Cyril Reenan met journalists from *The Sun* and played them extracts from a tape he had made of an explosive conversation. Though he didn't tell them what the material was before they pressed play, the journalists listened wide-eyed as they heard the unmistakeable voice of the Princess of Wales, engaged in an intimate conversation with an unidentified man. He was later identified as her close friend James Gilbey, who referred to her affectionately as Squidgy on the scandalous tapes.

The Sun published the story of the Squidgy tapes on 23 August 1992 and readers devoured the intimate chatter between the couple, which had been recorded on New Year's Eve in 1989. Though the princess's supporters dismissed the Squidgy bombshell as nothing more than an affectionate nickname between friends, Diana's anxious admission that she was worried she might fall pregnant was less easy to explain away. With the public hungry for more, the newspaper even made the original audio available on a premium rate number, which the princess herself called.

It was only after Squidgygate that it occurred to the Merseyside radio ham that there might be money in his recording. He took it to the *Daily Mirror* in autumn 1992 and was paid £30,000 for the tape. Perhaps most surprisingly of all given the reputation of the tabloid press for showing no mercy, the newspaper decided not to publish the tapes immediately . Instead, they kept them stored away until it became clear that the Wales' marriage was doomed. Satisfied now that its bosses wouldn't be labelled homewreckers, the *Mirror*'s editor, Richard Stott, decided to run with the story. The *Sunday People* and *Sunday Mirror* both published the full transcript on 17 January 1993.

The fallout from the publication of both the Charles and Diana transcripts tapes led to a formal investigation into how the telephone calls had been intercepted. Though the spotlight turned on the possible involvement of the security services, they were eventually cleared of any involvement. The radio hams, it seemed, really had got very lucky indeed. The newspaper revelations about the Prince and Princess of Wales, not to mention the unexpurgated transcripts and recordings of private telephone calls, were the first time that private royal business had become so devastatingly public. And that same public couldn't get enough of it.

The resultant scandal was enormous and particularly damaging for the Prince of Wales, who had already been rocked by the revelations contained in Andrew Morton's *Diana: Her True Story*. Charles became the subject of jokes, derision and disgust, with polls suggesting that his reputation and the public's respect for him had plummeted to an all-time low. Most of this disgust centred around the oft-misquoted moment in the call when, it was suggested by the press, he had said his greatest wish was to be Camilla's tampon. In actual fact, as the full transcripts and, to be fair, *The Crown*, show, the conversation was actually a light-hearted and affectionate exchange between lovers on what they thought was a private phone line. Was it cringy and clumsy? Yes. Was it the extreme perversion some tried to suggest? Nowhere near.

Just as viewers saw in *The Way Ahead*, in the wake of the resultant scandal, the embattled Prince of Wales consented to participate in a TV special in which he would be interviewed by Jonathan Dimbleby. Airing in June 1994, *Charles: The Private Man, the Public Role,* allowed the prince his own stage to talk about his work, his philanthropic interests and, inevitably, his marriage. In the unsurprisingly sympathetic documentary, the prince admitted that whilst he had not been faithful, he had not transgressed until it became clear that his marriage was over. It was only one element of the feature length documentary, but it nevertheless eclipsed everything else he discussed.

Charles: The Private Man, the Public Role was aired on ITV on 29 June 1994; that same night, Princess Diana attended the Serpentine Gallery wearing her infamous "revenge dress". The following morning, coverage of the documentary and the princess's glamorous outing vied for the front pages, with the couple in competition for the support of the nation. The War of the Waleses was on.

5.6 Ipatiev House

The Crown

In 1917, Queen Mary and George V are asked by the government to authorise a rescue mission that will save Tsar Nicholas II and his family from punishment at the hands of Russian revolutionaries; the king gives his wife the casting vote. With all hope of sanctuary lost, the family are abandoned to their fate. At Ipatiev House, in the darkest depths of the night, the Imperial family are murdered.

In 1992, meanwhile, Boris Yeltsin pays a visit to Buckingham Palace and issues a reciprocal invitation to the queen to visit Moscow. Her Majesty advises Yeltsin that since it was he who gave the order to demolish Ipatiev House, she will make the visit only if the remains of the Romanov family are exhumed from the site and given a proper burial. When Yeltsin consents, Prince Philip gives a sample of his DNA in order to identify the remains once and for all.

During their state visit to Russia, the queen and the Duke of Edinburgh acknowledge that they have grown apart and Philip admits that he now regards Penny as his closest friend. In an effort to strengthen her marriage, Elizabeth invites Penny to join the family on a public engagement.

The Truth

As we've already addressed, *The Crown* takes an occasionally peculiar line when it comes to the presentation of its female protagonists, and never more so than here. There is no historical basis whatsoever in Ipatiev House's assertion that Queen Mary kiboshed the rescue of the doomed Romanovs, whose slaughter is shown in counterpoint to the royal family enjoying a shooting party. Seven members of the Romanov dynasty died that in that slaughter. Alongside the Tsar and Tsarina and their five children, four loyal members of their household were also murdered. As the bodies of the Imperial family are disposed of, a stone-faced Queen Mary inspects the tally of the hunt, heartless to the last.

There is some truth in these opening scenes, but Queen Mary's heartless rejection of the family's rescue isn't an example of it. Sadly, the accuracy here comes with the dramatisation of the Romanovs' fate at Ipatiev House in Yekaterinburg. As 16 July 1918 drew to a close, the family were herded into the basement and, in the early hours of the following day, murdered by bullet and bayonet.

In the episode's prologue it's suggested that there was a chance that they might have been saved if King George had given his consent to mount a rescue mission. Whilst the government did seek the permission of George V (who did breakfast with a pet parrot on his shoulder) to mount a rescue operation, he didn't give his wife the right of veto. In fact, George, who was exceptionally close to his cousin, Tsar Nicholas II, was placed in an impossible position. There was no chance the Tsar would be restored to the throne and with World War I raging, Britain had to establish and maintain good relations with the incoming Bolshevik regime. To be seen as offering partisan support to the deposed Imperial family would have done untold damage to this new relationship. Not only that, but Tsarina Alexandra was German and enthusiastically supported the German cause in the war. To offer the Tsarina sanctuary at the very moment when Britain was at war against her home land was simply untenable. Crucially, there's no reason to believe that it was Queen Mary who held the deciding vote, nor that she coldly abandoned the Romanovs mere days before their murder.

If that wasn't irritating enough, Penny Knatchbull's theory that Mary feared Tsarina Alexandra would steal her limelight because she was prettier and more popular is cringingly annoying. Penny points out to the queen that Mary had been jealous of Alexandra's beauty and popularity since their girlhood in Germany. In fact, says Penny, Mary's late fiancé had only proposed to her after Alexandra turned him down. Stung by the knowledge that she was second best, suggests *The Crown*, Mary exacted her revenge in ice cold style.

It's nonsense. Mary and Alexandra did not grow up together and, though Alexandra did refuse the Duke of Clarence's proposal, there was no rivalry between the two women. Indeed, Mary's subsequent marriage to King George V was a loving one. The decision to reduce history down to the vagaries of female jealousy does a disservice not only to the characters and the truth, but to the viewer. Happily, it is left to the queen to espouse a more appropriate theory, when she tells Lady Romsey that it had nothing to do with women at war, but everything to do with international politics in the heat of a world war.

It's certainly no coincidence that it's the queen's apparent rival, Penny Knatchbull, who suggests that Queen Mary was jealous of a younger, glamourous woman. Naturally, it's Queen Elizabeth who posits the second theory, silencing her rival with her more considered, stateswomanly reading of the situation. The only thing is, Her Majesty and Penny Knatchbull were never in competition at all; their depiction as rivals for the attentions of the Duke of Edinburgh is entirely make believe.

And so to Yeltsin. It's accurate that Queen Elizabeth II made a state visit to Moscow in 1994, a trip that was hailed as a momentous thawing between Russia and the west. However, she did not do so only on condition that the remains of the Romanovs be exhumed and reburied. Also likely fictional is the rather questionable depiction of Yeltsin as a boorish drunk, spouting insults about the queen in Russian virtually to her face, well aware that she cannot understand what he is saying. Whilst Yeltsin was known to be a heavy drinker and certainly had his headline-grabbing moments of chaos, he was also a statesman. It's stretching credibility to suggest that he spent his official visit to the United Kingdom in an offensive, alcoholic haze, liberally showering his hosts with Russian oaths.

Another accurate beat in the script is the claim that the responsibility for the demolition of Ipatiev House was Yeltsin's. Whilst it wasn't solely his decision to pull down the building, which had become a place of pilgrimage for pro-Imperialists, he was the chair of the local branch of the Communist Party in Yekaterinburg as the number of pilgrims swelled. As the Politburo prepared to mark the 60th anniversary of the revolution in 1977, it was decided that the house should be demolished and responsibility for overseeing the works fell to Boris Yeltsin. It was not a task he took any pride in. Today, the Church of the Blood stands on the site and a cross marks the place where the family died.

Though this episode is a mix of truth and fiction, Prince Philip's involvement in the identification of the human remains found at Yekaterinburg was real. His maternal grandmother was the late Tsarina's sister and the duke gave a DNA sample that allowed scientists to confirm once and for all that they had discovered the remains of some of the tragic Imperial family. The remains of the Tsar and Tsarina and three of their daughters, along with their staff, were finally given a proper burial in 1998, eight decades after they were murdered. In 2007, the bodies of the two remaining Romanov children were found; they have yet to be laid to rest.

Finally, I think we can safely assume that the tense heart to heart between the royal couple about Penny is fiction. What's a season of *The Crown* without some angst for Prince Philip, after all?

5.7 No Woman's Land

The Crown

Panorama's Martin Bashir wins the confidence of Earl Spencer, Diana's brother, and convinces him that the Princess of Wales's household staff are being paid by the security services to spy on her. Earl Spencer introduces Diana to Bashir, who offers her the opportunity to film an interview with *Panorama* in which she can set the record straight and tell her story.

As William, by now a student at Eton, confides in the queen that he is concerned for his mother, Diana is trying to move on. She meets surgeon Hasnat Khan and a tentative romance begins.

The Truth

So, Martin Bashir. There's probably nobody watching *The Crown* who isn't very aware of Martin Bashir and the fallout from his *Panorama* interview that continues to this very day.

Ambitious journalist Bashir met Earl Spencer, Diana's brother, in summer 1995, a time when Diana was feeling more isolated than ever within the royal family. During this meeting Bashir showed Spencer evidence that his telephone was being bugged and that members of both his and Diana's household, including her trusted and unquestionably loyal private secretary, Patrick Jephson, were being paid by Britain's security services and possibly the Prince of Wales to keep tabs on the Spencer family and report their movements to shadowy and threatening paymasters. As we and Earl Spencer now know, the evidence presented by Bashir was fake and his shocking revelations were nothing but lies. And it wasn't just one or two lies either, but a complex web of them, supported by fraudulent records, bank statements and other fabricated paperwork specifically designed to mislead the princess and her family and earn their trust. The plan worked and eventually Earl Spencer was so taken in by the overwhelming weight of the fraudulent evidence that he introduced Bashir to Diana, just as *The Crown* depicts.

Once again, the journalist rolled out his lies and fraud, including a fake receipt that indicated the Prince of Wales had paid for the couple's nanny to have an abortion after she became pregnant with his child. Just like her brother, Diana was reeled in hook, line and sinker by Bashir's lies, unaware that she was the victim of an elaborate fraud. Already anxious that she was being watched, Bashir exploited the princess's frailties mercilessly. Under his malign influence she consented to her now infamous interview with *Panorama*. As the next episode will show, it hit the royal family like a bomb.

The second strand of this episode is Diana's burgeoning relationship with Dr Hasnat Khan. Just as *No Woman's Land* suggests, Diana met the doctor when she accompanied her friend and therapist, Oonagh Toffolo, to visit her husband during his treatment at Royal Brompton Hospital. This was the start of a relationship that lasted until 1997 and did include an incognito trip to see *Apollo 13*, as shown in *No Woman's Land*. Indeed, Diana also made a visit to Khan's family in Pakistan in 1996 which, perhaps surprisingly, we don't see on-screen. What we do see is Diana's deepening paranoia, fuelled by her isolation and stoked by Martin Bashir's falsehoods. Just as viewers witness, as the princess grew more dependent on Bashir, she even feared that someone might have tampered with the brakes on her car. Tragically, with the journalist encouraging and heightening her anxiety, she became ever more isolated and afraid until she relied on a very small number of close confidantes and a few trusted members of staff. By undermining even these relationships, such as that with Jephson, Bashir alienated the struggling princess still further. His actions would have enormous and long-term ramifications.

Finally, scenes depicting Prince William and Her Majesty bonding over their shared experience of Eton, where she received lessons as a young princess, perfectly reflect her loving and supportive relationship with her grandson. Whilst we obviously cannot know the content of William's discussions when his grandmother as his mother came under increasing stress, it doesn't seem so far-fetched that he would have discussed his worries with her. There's no doubt that Diana was at pains to give her sons a loving and supportive upbringing, and to help them live as normal a life as possible for boys who were born princes; it is something William and Harry recall with love to this day.

5.8 Gunpowder

The Crown

As Diana's relationship with Hasnat Khan goes from strength to strength, BBC Director General John Birt approves Martin Bashir's request to interview the Princess of Wales, but Earl Spencer has begun to doubt Bashir's version of events. His second thoughts come too late and even though he tries to warn his sister off, Diana decides to press ahead. The interview takes place on Bonfire Night beneath a veil of secrecy.

When Birt sees the programme he begins to wonder if it should be screened at all, but the broadcast goes ahead on what is, coincidentally, the queen's wedding anniversary. On the eve of the broadcast, Diana finally tells Elizabeth all about the interview. Things could hardly get any worse.

The Truth

"Even the televisions are metaphors in this place" grumbles Her Majesty as her knackered old TV set begins to break down. It's on the nose, but at least it's an acknowledgement that we're all on the same page.

And then there's *Panorama*. Titled *An Interview with HRH The Princess of Wales*, the now infamous 54-minute programme aired on 20 November 1995 and was watched by 200 million viewers across the world. Filmed secretly in Kensington Palace by a crew who smuggled in their equipment under the cover of installing a new hi-fi system, it launched Martin Bashir into a stratospheric international television career. It was a career that ended in disgrace.

In the programme, Diana discussed her unhappy marriage, the unceasing glare of the media spotlight and her experiences with depression, self-harm and bulimia. It was during this interview that she famously said "there were three of us in this marriage, so it was a bit crowded", arguably still one of the most quoted lines of the 1990s. Though she didn't mention Camilla by name, she didn't need to: Bashir did. The princess admitted her own affair with James Hewitt, which she put down to the pain of her loveless and miserable marriage and the royal family's cold rejection of her when she needed them most. Diana claimed that she had been deeply in love Hewitt, whose decision to sell his story left her devastated and betrayed. Abandoned by her husband, alienated by his family and treated as though she was mad, the embattled princess had apparently lurched from crisis to crisis. In an interview that was filled with revelations, one of the few bright spots came when she discussed her children, whom she obviously adored. The princess's apparent candour captured the hearts of the viewing public, even as it turned that same public against the Windsors.

Needless to say, Charles and Camilla did not come out of it well. The Parker Bowles divorced early in 1995 and by autumn Charles and Camilla were tentatively stepping out together with trusted friends. Whether they would have been quite so passionately demonstrative with one another as *Gunpowder* suggests is unlikely. The couple were making particular efforts to keep their relationship low-key for understandable reasons, but here they lock lips as fireworks light up the sky, little suspecting that Diana is busy filming the interview that will light a particularly inflammatory fuse. Subtle *The Crown* ain't.

Though Martin Bashir used the interview as a springboard for other high profile projects, questions over the circumstances in which he had secured the scoop wouldn't go away. A BBC inquiry in 1996 cleared Bashir of any wrongdoing but in 2020, the 25th anniversary of the broadcast saw a renewed interest in the interview and an avalanche of new documentaries and new enquiries followed. The BBC subsequently apologised to Earl Spencer for the use of forged documents that wrongly accused loyal and blameless members of the earl and princess's staff of being spies. Bashir, who had been rehired by the BBC in 2016, left the Corporation in 2021, his reputation in tatters. The BAFTA which the programme had won was returned.

As *Gunpowder* accurately reflects, Diana's *Panorama* interview dropped a depth charge on the traditionally cordial relationship between the BBC and the royal family. The clash between the traditionalist chairman of the Beeb, Sir Marmaduke Hussey, and the modernising Director-General, John Birt, that is depicted in this episode serves a dual purpose. On the one hand, it emphasises the way in which the institution was changing and leaving the old guard behind, adopting what seemed to some to be a more savage and merciless approach than was typical. The BBC governors were actually kept in the dark about the interview until it was too late to turn back, as Birt knew that

Hussey's close ties to the royal family might well cause him to try to step in: Lady Hussey was even one of the queen's ladies-in-waiting. Hussey later admitted that the interview with Diana had cast a pall over the final months that led up to his retirement from the Chairmanship, though contrary to what *Gunpowder* suggests, he did not offer his resignation to the queen in person. Instead, he retired as he had already been intending to do.

The clash between Hussey and Birt isn't just symbolic of the two sides of the BBC at war, it's also another one of those metaphors that *The Crown* so loves. Sir Marmaduke Hussey is the old, John Birt the new, just as the traditional old royal Firm is under fire from the trailblazing Diana, who is a very different sort of royal to any that has gone before. It's no coincidence that as the Princess of Wales prepares to send a shockwave through the House of Windsor, Prince William's class at Eton are receiving a lecture on Guy Fawkes's efforts to remove the old order and replace it with the new. What a gift to the programme makers that Diana filmed her interview on 5 November.

Though we don't usually get into the minutiae of days of the week, it's worth noting that 5 November 1995 was a Sunday; portentous though Prince William's lesson might be, there are no classes at Eton on Sunday. A similar bit of dramatic license occurs when the episode shows the interview being broadcast on Charles's birthday. But Charles's birthday falls on 14 November, whereas the interview was broadcast almost a week later on 20 November. Despite this date discrepancy, *Gunpowder* accurately portrays Elizabeth and Philip not watching the interview, but attending the Royal Variety Performance instead. Not much of a trade up.

Though *Gunpowder* shows the Princess of Wales informing the queen of the interview on the day before it airs, that would appear to be conjecture. The palace learned of the broadcast six days before it was due to go on. Whilst we will never be privy to the private reaction of Her Majesty, the relationship between the royal family and Princess Diana unsurprisingly grew more frosty than ever once word of the interview got out. Until then Diana had enjoyed the friendship of Prince Philip and Princess Margaret, who had not been half as forgiving to Sarah Ferguson when her transgressions were made public, but the *Panorama* interview ended this for good. By telling Bashir and the world that she couldn't say if Prince Charles was a good candidate to be king,

Diana had crossed the line: she had cast doubt on the succession itself. However, whilst the family drew in a collective breath and closed ranks, the public outpouring of support for Diana was almost overwhelming. She had wanted to tell her version of her story and when she did, people rallied to her side.

Prince William and Prince Harry have both addressed the documentary in recent years, speaking frankly about the way in which Bashir contributed to their mother's overwhelming isolation and distress. They, along with Prince Charles, received written apologies from the BBC, whilst a BBC employee whose career had been ruined after Bashir made him the scapegoat for the fraud received a substantial settlement. Further settlements were made with Tiggy Legge-Bourke, the royal nanny whom Bashir falsely claimed had aborted Charles's baby, and Patrick Jephson, whilst generous donations were made to charities close to the heart of the late Princess of Wales. Bashir also apologised, though he continued to claim that Diana's eventual decision to collaborate on the documentary was not influenced by any of the false statements or fake documents he had procured. The BBC has given its word that it will never air the interview again, nor allow other broadcasters to do so.

5.9 Couple 31

The Crown

The Queen writes to the Prince and Princess of Wales and advises them to divorce. Diana deals with the fallout of the *Panorama* interview and the end of her relationship with Hasnat Khan. With Charles and Diana unable to agree on settlement terms, the Queen asks John Major to act as an intermediary.

With an eye to one day making things official with Camilla, Charles retains PR executive Mark Bolland to help him navigate the challenges the couple will face as she increasingly becomes a part of his public life: he advises the prince to agree to Diana's terms so both parties can move on. Charles and Diana seem to have reached a ceasefire, but a companionable dinner turns into a bitter battle of words. Their divorce is finalised, but the story isn't over.

The Truth

After their separation was announced, the Prince and Princess of Wales reached a deadlock. Neither wanted to be married to the other, but equally neither wanted to be the one to make the first move towards a divorce. It was the queen who eventually told them that the time had come to make it official, though the letter she writes in *Couple 31* is, of course, an invention of the scriptwriter. In reality she wrote to advise Diana that she had spoken to Charles, the Archbishop of Canterbury, and John Major and that all agreed that a divorce was the only appropriate next move. Just before Christmas in 1995, the public learned that the marriage was at an end: divorce proceedings were underway.

At first, all had seemed rosy for Princess Diana and heart surgeon Hasnat Khan. The couple were friends for several weeks before Diana accompanied Khan on a visit to his aunt and uncle; following that, they became romantic partners. As things got more serious, Diana met Khan's family in Pakistan and introduced him to her sons; there was talk of marriage and a shared future. And then the *Sunday People* got involved. They broke the story of the affair in 1996 and Khan, who had until then lived a life away from any sort of spotlight, suddenly found himself under press and public scrutiny: it was more than he could bear. Things grew tense between the couple and when Diana began to see more of Dodi Fayed, Khan suspected there may be someone else in the picture. The princess denied that she was seeing another man, but broke off their relationship within days. Immediately afterwards, she flew to France to meet Dodi Fayed.

Whilst *The Crown* depicts Diana's relationship with Hasnat Khan coming to an end in the immediate wake of the *Panorama* broadcast, the couple actually stayed together until 1997. Despite long-standing rumours that Khan could no longer cope with the media intrusion that came with Diana and had therefore broken off the affair, he later confirmed that it was the princess who had ended the relationship. It was the last she saw of the man she had once told friends was "the love of my life".

Couple 31 claims that Charles hired Mark Bolland to help him and Camilla improve their joint public image as the prepared to go public, and there's certainly some truth in that. Bolland, who was hired in 1997 and worked for Charles as a Deputy Private Secretary for five years, was the first PR exec to take the royal family in hand. He has been credited with doing much of the heavy lifting that was required to massage Charles and Camilla's public image in the wake of the divorce. It was he who masterminded a meeting between the queen and Camilla during a party given at Highgrove in 2000 to celebrate the birthday of Constantine II. The meeting, which was regarded as hugely significant at the time, was widely and positively publicised thanks to Bolland's efforts and sent a clear signal that Her Majesty saw Camilla as a welcome and stabilising influence on the Prince of Wales. Following the divorce and the outpouring of public disapproval for Charles and Camilla, it was a shrewd move.

Whilst there was no doubt some wrangling over the divorce settlement, *The Crown*'s assertion that John Major resolved the deadlock is untrue. Major did try to offer the couple some advice at the time of the initial separation, but if he had any involvement in their divorce negotiations, he has understandably kept the matter confidential. It's far more likely, of course, that he simply wasn't involved. Amongst the terms of divorce was shared custody of the children, and an undisclosed financial settlement for Diana, though the figures used in this episode of a one-off payment of £17 million and an annual stipend of £400,000 have been rumoured for years. The princess was allowed to keep her apartments at Kensington Palace and enjoy free use of royal aircraft, but she didn't have it all her own way. No longer a member of the royal family, Diana relinquished her title of Her Royal Highness but retained that of Princess of Wales. As a side note, once the Prince of Wales and Camilla were married, she did not use the title of Princess of Wales, despite being entitled to do so. Instead, she was the Duchess of Cornwall: today, she is Queen Consort.

Just as the episode shows, the queen and John Major did enjoy a warm relationship, which blossomed during Her Majesty's infamous 1992 annus horribilis. It was a mark of her affection and respect for Major that he was appointed as special guardian to Prince William and Prince Harry following the death of their mother. Tellingly, he was the only former prime minister who received an invitation to the wedding of Prince Harry and Meghan Markle.

5.10 Decommissioned

The Crown

At the 1997 General Election, a massive Labour landslide sweeps Tony Blair into Downing Street. One of his first tasks is to tell the queen that he will not spend taxpayers' money on a new royal yacht and to suggest that she could use a privately owned vessel instead. As a result, Her Majesty decides to retire Britannia without replacing her.

During a trip to mark the handover of Hong Kong, Blair and Prince Charles have a frank discussion regarding the need to modernise the monarchy. The queen has a final moment with Britannia before the royal yacht is retired for good.

The Truth

In January 1997, Sir Trevor McDonald hosted a televised debate entitled *The Monarchy Debate – The Nation Decides*, in which a panel of experts discussed whether the monarchy should be abolished. The programme makers invited viewers to have their say by voting for or against the royal family via a premium rate telephone poll. *The Crown* depicts Diana obsessively voting against the monarchy, which is likely a touch of black humour more than anything else. Who could blame her, though?

We're back in metaphor land in this final episode of season five and, just as the season opened with discussion regarding the future of the Royal Yacht Britannia, so too will it close with the twilight of that famed vessel. The ship is to be decommissioned and, as the queen ruefully considers its fate, it doesn't take a genius to understand that she too is symbolic of Britannia: outdated, tired and no longer relevant in a modern world. This series of *The Crown* has really pushed this narrative of a monarch out of place and increasingly redundant in a changing world. Whether struggling to understand modern marriages or tussling with her Sky remote, we're constantly shown Elizabeth wondering whether she really belongs in the twenty-first century at all. Of course, there's no reason to suspect that Her Majesty really felt that way, but it certainly makes for some entertaining soap opera.

The 1997 fall of John Major's Tory government was spectacular, coming as it did courtesy of a landslide for the Labour Party. With the Conservative administration brought to its knees by the economic collapse of Black Wednesday, the embarrassing revelations that undermined its Back to Basics campaign, and vicious infighting over the issue of Europe, the electorate sent the Tories packing in dramatic style. Yet whilst his farewell scenes in *Decommissioned* show Major telling the queen that he believed he would be able to win the election, this was never the case. The former prime minister knew that the writing was on the wall after a tumultuous few months and later admitted that he was somewhat relieved to leave Downing Street forever. And who can blame him? The incoming prime minister, Tony Blair, came to office riding a wave of public approval. His immense popularity on assuming office didn't last. Blair later recalled that when he attended his first audience at Buckingham Palace, he invited the monarch to call him Tony. She declined to do so.

Whilst the fate of the queen in this latest run of episodes has been that of a relic who no longer understands the world around her, Charles seems destined to remain frustrated at his mother's resistance to modernise the institution that she represents. During a clandestine meeting with Tony Blair during the handover of Hong Kong, Charles admits that he is tormented by the family's lack of appetite for modernisation. In an effort to stoke up the drama, *Decommissioned* suggests that such a meeting between the Prince of Wales and the prime minster is inappropriate and unconstitutional, but it really isn't: there would be no scandal in the heir to the throne meeting the PM to discuss constitutional affairs. After all, he's going to be sitting on the throne himself one day. Also fabricated are the scenes in which Camilla and Charles take a romantic cruise on board Britannia once the prince's duty in Hong Kong is concluded. Far from being joined by his lover, in reality Charles immediately departed for an official visit to the Philippines before returning to England with Chris Patten, the last governor of Hong Kong. Not quite the romantic interlude that *The Crown* would have us believe.

Britannia took her final voyage in July 1997, arriving in Hong Kong to serve as a base for Prince Charles during the official handover celebrations. Interestingly, the scene that depicts Charles flying in business class whilst the politicians and other dignitaries are in first is accurate. What isn't true is that he knew about it beforehand: he only found out once he was safely in his seat. Needless to say, it wasn't Charles's decision.

There is more veracity in the scenes that show Dodi Fayed with his girlfriend, model Kelly Fisher. According to Fisher, Dodi had proposed to her and given her a ring, so she was taken by surprise to learn that he was seeing Diana on the side. Of course, so far Diana and Dodi have yet to meet in *The Crown*, but we all know that the day is coming and when Diana heads off on holiday with Al-Fayed at the end of this episode, that day moves ever closer. Mohamed Al-Fayed invited the princess to bring Prince William and Prince Harry to holiday on his yacht and at his estate in the south of France, apparently because he was concerned about the lonely life she seemed to live. When the party arrived, photographers clustered along the shoreline in the hope of snapping a photo that would prove that rumours of a relationship between Dodi and the princess were true. The undercurrent in *Decommissioned*, as Al-Fayed boorishly advises his son that Kelly Fisher is good only for sex, is that he's set his ruthless sights on matchmaking Dodi with the Princess of Wales.

Tony Blair, whose relationship with the queen was somewhat stiff, decided to decommission the Royal Yacht Britannia due to the same crippling costs of refurbishment her that had already scared John Major's government off the project. It was a decision he later came to bitterly regret. As seen on-screen, the possibility that the royal family could instead use a privately-owned vessel for their voyages was one of the options that were considered. Just as *Decommissioned* notes with relish, Blair rather liked the name New Britain.

Whilst *The Crown* has never shied away from creating drama and inserting overwrought emotions into scenes where it wasn't present, or even from rewriting history to suggest that the queen is lacking in emotions– *Aberfan*, anyone? – Elizabeth's sadness at the decommissioning of the royal yacht was very real. As she attended the ceremony, Her Majesty wiped a tear away in a rare public show of emotion. The queen, just like the rest of us, was human after all.

And so season five reaches its end. John Major is gone, the Princess of Wales is moving on and Charles is still trying to modernise the monarchy. This time, though, he hopes to do so with Camilla at his side. We'll see.

❆❅SEASON 6❆❅

6.1 Persona Non Grata

The Crown

A car speeds through night time Paris, pursued by a pack of photographers on motorcycles. It descends into the Pont de l'Alma tunnel and the sound of a wreck splits the night. In a flashback to a few weeks earlier, Prime Minister Tony Blair meets Princess Diana to discuss her wish for an official role; though Blair is sympathetic, the queen rejects the request. She also rejects Prince Charles's invitation to attend the party he is planning in celebration of Camilla's 50th birthday. To avoid press coverage of the party, Diana takes William and Harry to Saint-Tropez at the invitation of Mohamed Al-Fayed. After they are pursued by photographers, Diana strikes a bargain with the paparazzi that her children will be left alone if she lets them photograph her in her swimming costume.

Al-Fayed summons Dodi to Saint-Tropez, where he intends to matchmake his son with Diana, despite Dodi already being engaged. When Diana gets home, she finds an invitation to Paris from Dodi waiting for her.

The Truth

And so we find ourselves at what is supposedly the final season of *The Crown*, with the first four episodes covering weeks, not years. And what weeks they are; a period that shook the monarchy and kickstarted its modernisation. The sixth season attracted a storm of press coverage when it emerged that Diana would appear as a ghost, though in the event, she wasn't so much a spectre as a convenient narrative device, serving as a manifestation of Charles's inner turmoil and the queen's need to connect with her subjects rather than a phantom from the pages of MR James.

Another controversy centred on the depiction of the car crash that claimed the life of Diana, Dodi Fayed and chauffeur Henri Paul, and left security officer Trevor Rees-Jones with life-changing injuries. In the event, the wreck which occurs in the very first minutes of the first episode is kept off screen. We see only the car and its pursuers as they speed into the tunnel at the Pont de l'Alma, to be followed a moment later by the sound of a smash.

When the episode starts proper, it's with a flashback to Diana calling on Tony Blair at Chequers, where she asks him for some sort of official role that would make the best of her skills. This is accurate, as Diana did indeed visit the PM's country residence with Prince William in search of a job. Though Blair admitted there had been discussions about her role, he went onto recall that Diana had been left annoyed by the conversation, though he never disclosed exactly what it was that rubbed her the wrong way. It's a sort of half score for the series, though whether we'll ever see Cherie refuse to curtsey to the queen, as she did in real life, only time will tell (spoiler – we don't). One thing we certainly don't see is the prime minister personally expressing his concerns about Diana's close ties to Dodi Fayed during the meeting. This, in fact, is something the series notably chooses to avoid.

Whilst *The Crown* has much to say about Mohamed Al-Fayed's ceaseless and ultimately unsuccessful quest to British achieve citizenship, it doesn't delve into some of his shadier practices, particularly the now-infamous cash-for-questions affair. This occurred when Al-Fayed bribed two Conservative MPs to ask questions in Parliament and make other efforts to further his interests in the highest circles of government. It was a tawdry affair and tales of brown envelopes stuffed with cash provided rich pickings for satirists and journalists alike. The fallout shook the government and further undermined public confidence in the tottering Major administration, ultimately resulting in its trouncing when it came to election time. The revelation of such dodgy dealings only served to damage Mohamed Al-Fayed's reputation, leaving him further than ever from the British passport he so craved.

Intriguingly, whilst the episode depicts a steely-eyed queen telling Blair that Diana cannot be half in and half out of the family, Prince

Harry's own memoirs would suggest that there may be a grain of truth in the idea, if not the scene. Prince Harry had suggested a similar "half in, half out" arrangement for himself and his family, only to be told in no uncertain terms that it wasn't possible. The loudest opponent, according to the Duke of Sussex, was his father, Charles. It's not too far-fetched to imagine that Peter Morgan would've been well aware of these claims, especially since Harry revealed them in his own documentary series that was screened - where else? – but on Netflix.

Speaking of Prince Charles, he's still angsting; this time, the cause is his mother's refusal to accept Camilla or to attend her 50th birthday party. A party that, in real life, there was never any suggestion that she or any other royal would attend. After all, why would they? It was Camilla's celebration for her own family and friends, not her boyfriend's mother. On screen it's a glittering affair, despite Her Majesty's absence, with the prince reading an emotional speech from Jane Austen's *Persuasion* as guests including Princess Margaret look on misty-eyed. Margaret is so touched that she later telephones her sister to make a case on behalf of the couple, no doubt remembering her own devastating split with her true love, Peter Townsend, decades earlier.

The Crown always excels when it comes to recreating costumes, from the queen's wedding gown to Diana's engagement suit and now Camilla's Highgrove House party dress and jewellery. What it doesn't nail so well in this case is the guest list or the speeches. None of the royal family attended and Charles certainly didn't turn to Jane Austen for his inspiration. In fact, the only person who did address the guests was Camilla's son Tom, when he wished his mum a happy birthday and thanked the prince for playing host. Whilst Princess Margaret wasn't at the party, though, it's almost all we'll see of her in these first four episodes, so don't blink or you might miss her. In fact, blink half a dozen times this season and you might well miss the queen herself.

Whether Princess Margaret ever lobbied for the couple is open to conjecture, but she categorically wasn't at the party that night. Given the timeframe concerned, it's worth noting that it was in July 1997 that news of Charles and Camilla's shared wish to marry began to emerge, with newspapers across the globe sitting up and taking notice. Of course, events in Paris were to put a stop to this ambition for a long time,

Although these four episodes might feel like an exhaustive chronicle of the last eight weeks of Diana's life, not every significant incident is covered and there are a number of artistic liberties at play. There are also some notable omissions, most glaring being the lack of even a nod of acknowledgement to the murder of Diana's close friend, Gianni Versace. Versace was killed in July 1997, well within the scope of these episodes, but despite the fashion designer being a close friend of the princess, his death doesn't merit a mention. In point of fact, she was actually in the south of France as a guest of Al-Fayed when she received the tragic news.

Also missing from this episode, in which Diana's famous animal-print swimming costume is impressively recreated, is the press' obsession with the princess's physique during her sojourn to the south of France. At the time, when the papers were bursting with pictures of Diana in her swimsuit, some journalists speculated that she appeared to be pregnant. Diana was so furious that she reportedly told one journalist that she had cut the swimming costume to shreds. Yet none of these rumours make it into *The Crown*, perhaps because they might cloud the potential romance scriptwriters are building between Dodi and Diana; it's pretty much its own mini-series.

There are multiple takes on the relationship between Diana and Dodi but *The Crown* imagines the couple as unwitting pawns of the ambitious and scheming Al-Fayed, who believes a marriage between them will finally catapult him into the cream of British society. It is he who invites the princess and his unsuspecting son along to Saint-Tropez and conspires to bring them together with the ultimate goal of using their relationship to secure British citizenship. With Diana looking for a purpose in life and Dodi desperate to please his domineering father, they soon begin a tentative friendship, but Al-Fayed is intent on nothing less than a wedding.

First things first. Those close to Al-Fayed have for years refuted claims that he attempted to matchmake the couple in order to achieve British citizenship and have balked at the suggestion that it was he who secretly employed a photographer to capture apparently clandestine photos of the couple kissing. However, Al-Fayed did invite the princess and her sons to holiday with him at his villa and when the party moved to his yacht, the Jonikal, it was he who invited Dodi along. Beyond that, scenes in which he leans heavily on his son to win Diana's heart would appear to be fictional. Not fictional is the watch Dodi sends Diana, one of several expensive gifts he gave the princess during their brief relationship.

Also open to question is the depiction of model Kelly Fisher as Dodi's fiancée. Fisher, a model who met Dodi in Paris in July 1996, claimed after he was photographed with the princess that she had been engaged to him since February 1997. It was a claim that the Al-Fayed family later denied, but one that *The Crown* takes as gospel. The scenes depicting Kelly ensconced on a neighbouring yacht to the Jonikal, however, are true: Dodi really was jaunting back and forth between the two as he was getting to know the Princess of Wales. Whilst in the series Fisher fears losing her fiancé to Diana before she even sets off to join him in the Mediterranean sunshine, in reality, she claimed to have no idea that Diana was on the neighbouring yacht, nor that her boyfriend was heading off each day to spend time with her. We'll see more, though not much more, of Fisher later in this first tranche of four episodes; like so many others, she's very much a bit player here.

6.2 Two Photographs

The Crown

The royal family is shaken by reports of Diana's secret weekend in Paris with Dodi, fearing Al-Fayed will use it as leverage in his efforts to obtain British citizenship. Hoping to put pressure on his son to take the relationship further, Al-Fayed secretly arranges for the couple to be photographed in a clinch. It sparks a record-breaking bidding war. When Diana visits Bosnia to call for a ban on landmines, she finds her efforts to raise awareness frustrated by the media obsession over her private life.

Charles agrees to a photo shoot with William and Harry at Balmoral, as the queen and Prince Philip reflect on Diana's attention-grabbing behaviour.

The Truth

Photographers Mario Brenna and Duncan Muir are the early focus of this episode. They are very different types: one glamorous and wealthy, the other staid and respectful. One real, one fictional.

Mario Brenna is indeed a celebrity photographer of some renown, whose front-page A-list images command a premium, largely thanks to his infamous snap of the Princess of Wales. Yet whilst it was he who captured the first grainy images of Dodi and Diana's embraces on board the yacht, he was not doing so at the secret behest of Mohamed Al-Fayed. In fact, Al-Fayed gets a particularly rough ride in these episodes of *The Crown*, presented as a domineering, manipulative schemer who uses his son and the princess as pawns in his campaign to gain the British passport that was destined to remain forever out of his reach. He is depicted interrogating staff to find out if the couple are sharing a bed, cajoling, bullying and plotting to get his hands on the prize without a thought for the two people at the heart of the plot. All of this, it's worth remembering, is conjecture at best. Despite fevered speculation, Brenna has always insisted that he was nobody's hired hand.

But there is truth in this episode too. There's no question that Diana was hounded by paparazzi during her trip to Saint-Tropez and that Brenna's photographs poured fuel on the fire. Some commentators have understandably asked just how it was that Brenna tracked down the Jonikal in the Med, but there's very little mystery there. Whilst *Two Photographs* shows Al-Fayed leaking the yacht's location and manifest, if any such leak even existed it's far more like to have come from a crew member.

In fact, Brenna himself has said that he and Al-Fayed had no secret deal and that the truth about his being in the right place at the right time wasn't down to anything more sinister than force of habit. Every summer, he stationed himself on the glitzy shores of the Mediterranean, snapping unsuspecting A-listers as they lived it up in the sunshine. He happened upon Diana and Dodi not by design, but purely by accident: the Jonikal was just one more super yacht in a sea filled with them. Nor did he grab the photos that made his name without working for them either. Once he realised who he had stumbled upon, finding the perfect vantage point and capturing the moment that the world saw was a matter of both careful preparation and a serious helping of luck.

Just as *The Crown* depicts, Brenna, who had no involvement in the episode and disagrees with its depiction of him as a metaphorical "killer", spent days on the tail of the vessel, hiking up clifftops until he found the ideal spot from which to get the pictures that captured the imagination of a public hungry for gossip. Though *Two Photographs* intimates that the paparazzo was already wealthy when he got the shots, he was anything but: the pictures he took that day in the Mediterranean are what made his fortune and catapulted him to the pinnacle of the paparazzi pack. Brenna later admitted that, in the months after the *Sunday Mirror* first published the photographs, he made almost £2 million from those right place, right time images. That figure would only climb.

Duncan Muir, meanwhile, is one of the more curious creations of Peter Morgan and his creative team. He seems to be the almost perfect royal photographer: low key, deferential, old-school and entirely fictional. Muir may well have been inspired by Arthur Edwards, a royal enthusiast who has photographed members of the House of Windsor for decades and who, in spring 2023, surprised royal-watchers when Catherine, Princess of Wales, greeted him warmly after spotting him in a crowd. Whilst Muir isn't Edwards, he represents the same respectful sort of royal watching that his real-life counterpart embodies.

And then we come to Balmoral. Whilst Charles, William and Harry did indeed agree to a photocall whilst at their Scottish retreat that summer, those photographs weren't captured by one forelock-tugging local, but by a press pack numbering in excess of three dozen professional Fleet Street snappers. Nor was it miserable and wet, the polar opposite of Saint-Tropez glamour, but a bright, sunny day. The intention of the scriptwriters is clear: the royal family live a life of tradition, of kilts in the Highlands and soggy photoshoots. Yet whilst Diana may have cornered the market in glamour, she pays for it with her privacy.

Similarly, whilst *The Crown* posits that Charles agreed to the photographs as a clapback at Diana's own courting of the press, it's far more likely that this Balmoral photocall was actually a quid pro quo between royals and photographers. As a matter of routine, the family have often agreed to arranged shoots in return for privacy during their holidays and continue to do so today.

Whilst most of this episode is taken up with soap opera-esque foreshadowing of tragedy, it does find time to touch on occasional moments of truth. Diana did made a trip to Bosnia in support of her campaign for an outright ban on landmines, though there was no unruly press conference at which questions regarding her sex life overwhelmed the message she was hoping to get across. Additionally, though her work was on behalf of the Landmine Survivors' Network, the charity emblem she wears in *Two Photographs* is a fictional one. There is also a little inevitable squishing together of the timeline, with Diana's famous minefield walk in Angola in January 1997 being transplanted to her trip to Bosnia instead. Whilst the photos of her canoodling with Dodi cause chaos at her Bosnian press conference, she was actually already home by the time they hit the front pages.

Whether the queen really was sniffy about Diana's penchant for psychics and their ilk is open to debate, but it's not impossible to imagine. Definitely accurate is the soapy angle of Kelly Fisher launching a case for breach of contract against Dodi when the snaps of him and the Princess of Wales were published. Fisher gave a teary, Dynasty-esque press conference with her lawyer, Gloria Allred, flashing a sparkling engagement ring as she told the world's press that her heart had been broken. She also claimed that her career had been irreparably damaged, as she had consented to Dodi's request to abandon her modelling career and focus instead on their relationship and forthcoming marriage: his betrayal had wrecked the plans she alleged that they had made together. Fisher sold her story to Rupert Murdoch for a reported £200,000 and after Dodi's death, claimed that she had expected to become his wife that very month. The Al-Fayed family dismissed her claims out of hand and Fisher dropped her lawsuit, leaving Allred to explain that she had done so out of respect for their loss.

6.3 Dis-Moi Oui

The Crown

Dodi plans to propose to Diana in Paris. Diana arrives in the French capital intent on speaking to her sons, but instead she is dragged around the city with the paparazzi in pursuit. After a stop-off at the Villa Windsor, she finally calls the boys. To Diana's surprise, William asks her if she and Dodi will marry; she answers with an emphatic no.

When Dodi proposes at the Ritz, Diana gently explains that she isn't ready for marriage and instead the couple talk about what has brought them to this point. Dodi can't bring himself to either confirm or deny the engagement when he speaks to his father, but instead tells him cryptically that an agreement was reached. The couple speed away from the Ritz with bodyguard Trevor Rees-Jones; hotel employee Henri Paul is at the wheel. During the fraught journey through Paris, the car crashes.

The Truth

So here we are at arguably the most anticipated and controversial episode of *The* Crown so far. In an episode heavy with fiction and imagined conversations, Peter Morgan finally arrives at the night of Princess Diana's death. By necessity, given that most of the action depicted in *Dis-Moi Oui* happened behind closed doors, there is a huge amount of dramatic license. Let's see how it stacks up against what truth we know.

In *Dis-Moi Oui*, Diana is bored. She is finding Dodi's efforts at romance touching yet cringy and longs for just one thing: to be back with her sons. In telephone conversations with her therapist, the princess acknowledges that drama is an addiction that she is desperate to break. Caught in the whirlwind chaos of the South of France, Diana makes up her mind: she will go home to her children tomorrow.

Despite Diana's determination, she finds herself dragged from one chaotic episode to another, beginning that evening with a trip to Monte Carlo. Though trying to pass unnoticed, crowds are soon pursuing the princess, Dodi and their security officer, Trevor Rees-Jones. They find sanctuary in a branch of jewellery store Repossi, where Diana's absent-minded admiration of an engagement ring sets Dodi on a fateful path.

This chase that leads to the jewellery shop didn't happen, though Mohamed Al-Fayed later claimed that the couple had indeed visited a jeweller in Monte Carlo on the night before they went to Paris. Furthermore, at the inquest into Diana's death, the jury saw CCTV footage of Dodi paying for a £12,000 ring bearing the words "Dis-moi Oui" from a Repossi store across the square from the Ritz in Paris; this ring was later brought to the hotel by an employee. The receipt for the purchase confirmed that it was an engagement ring, though that's not confirmation that Dodi had intended to propose that night. However, he had ordered the trinket over a week earlier, not the night before as depicted in *The Crown*.

As shown on screen, the princess and Dodi went immediately to the Villa Windsor upon their arrival in Paris, with photographers in constant pursuit. Though the trip had been more or less impromptu, the couple decided to leave the coast after an altercation in the waters around the yacht with yet more paparazzi. Fed up with the intrusion, they elected to spend their last evening before Diana's trip home in Paris. Her decision to leave for England wasn't taken on a whim, but had been planned from the start. She had no intention of remaining indefinitely in the Mediterranean.

Incidentally, Diana had also received another ring from Dodi before the rumoured Paris proposal, which she wore on her right hand as a friendship ring. But does this mean it was a love affair for the ages? Not really; what it proves is that there was a relationship of some sort between the couple and that they valued each other's company. Whilst Al-Fayed and Dodi's family later told the world that the couple were in love and intended to marry, it's something that we will never know for sure. Al-Fayed himself initially claimed that Dodi had told him on the night he died that he and Diana were betrothed, but later admitted that he wasn't sure if the proposal had happened already or was imminent. After Diana's death, her friends said that the princess was revelling in her newly single life; whilst she was enjoying spending time with Dodi, she reportedly told her pals that she needed another marriage like she needed a facial rash.

Diana was due back in the UK on 31 August and, just as the episode shows, did speak to her sons from Paris. Though they have not revealed the content of that last conversation, both have expressed their regret about how brief it was; understandably, it's a memory they have preferred to keep private. On the subject of the boys, whilst Diana is shown wrapping a PlayStation for Harry, the prince recalled that he received an Xbox that his mother had purchased before her death. However, this console wasn't released until four years later. Equally worth noting is the fact that William's blooding, the practice of smearing the blood of a hunter's first kill on the hunter's face, took place a year earlier, rather than on the eve of Diana's death. *The Crown* never could resist a symbolic stag.

After a guided tour of the former home of the Duke and Duchess of Windsor that did not, as far as we know, include a telephone call in which Al-Fayed promised the villa to Diana if she and Dodi stayed together, the couple headed off to the Ritz. They were accompanied by Rees-Jones and two drivers, one of whom was Henri Paul, assistant director of security at the Al-Fayed-owned Ritz Paris. They found the hotel besieged by photographers, scenes which were repeated first when they arrived at Dodi's apartment later that evening and again when they set out for dinner in Rue Saint-Martin.

Thanks to the paparazzi who swarmed around them, Dodi and Diana never made it to their chosen restaurant; instead, they decided to eat at the Ritz. Viewers of *Dis-Moi Oui* saw them forced to leave their table after other diners stared relentlessly and this did indeed happen. Tired of feeling like goldfish in a bowl, they instead sought sanctuary in the Imperial Suite, intending to return to Dodi's apartment after dinner. This, of course, is where speculation must take over. Whatever conversation took place between Diana and Dodi will remain a mystery, but *The Crown* suggests that the princess rebuffed Dodi's proposal, before the couple went on to spend hours in deep and affectionate conversation, each counselling the other. Revelling in this new-found honesty and freedom, Dodi tells Diana that she must slow down, whilst she advises him that he should finally stand up to his father. The viewer is left in no doubt that this was a relationship that both cherished, even if wasn't one that was going to lead to marriage just yet.

In a subsequent telephone conversation with Dodi, Fayed is desperate to know if Diana accepted his proposal. Dodi tells his father only that the couple reached an agreement; what that agreement was, he never says. Instead, he hangs up on Al-Fayed in an uncharacteristic demonstration of rebellion against his domineering father. Of course, once Dodi is dead, Al-Fayed sets out to convince the world that the couple were engaged.

Though this conversation is fictional, what happened next is all too tragically real. Believing that he had finished his shift for the night, Henri Paul had spent the evening drinking before he was called back to work. *The Crown* opts to show him in the bar of the Ritz, but there are multiple conflicting testimonies regarding where and with whom he had spent the evening. What is beyond dispute is that he had been drinking heavily and shouldn't have been behind the wheel. In order to let Diana and Dodi escape unseen, the hotel security created a decoy intended to confuse the waiting photographers. Namely, the cars the couple had travelled in earlier that day would wait at the hotel's front entrance, whilst the party would exit via the back door and slip into a different vehicle, driven by Henri Paul. They left at 12.20 am; only Trevor Rees-Jones was definitely wearing a seatbelt.

At first, the photographers fell for the plot, but once the couple's car was noticed by the waiting press, a pack of paparazzi on mopeds took off in pursuit. At the head of the chase was the speeding Mercedes, desperately attempting to outrun the flashbulbs as it dropped down into the four lane underpass at Place de l'Alma. Paul lost control of the vehicle just inside the tunnel, resulting in a catastrophic smash. He and Dodi were killed instantly; Diana was alive but more seriously injured than initial reports suggested, whilst Rees-Jones, the sole survivor, suffered life-changing injuries. Wisely, neither the crash nor its immediate aftermath are shown on screen.

6.4 Aftermath

The Crown

Dodi and Henri Paul are dead, whilst Diana is undergoing surgery that will ultimately prove unsuccessful. As Al-Fayed goes to Paris to retrieve his son's body, Charles gently breaks the tragic news to his sons. Al-Fayed sends gifts, letters and the late princess's possessions to the royal family, but receives no acknowledgement. A poem he asks to be placed in her coffin is returned. He feels utterly rejected.

Charles flies to Paris to accompany Diana's coffin home. At Balmoral, the queen refuses to pander to the public outcry over the death of the princess and focuses instead on her grandchildren, despite Charles's warnings that the family is making a mistake. However, as the clamour grows, she recants and agrees to a ceremonial funeral for Diana, against the Duke of Edinburgh's advice. Though he warns that they must adhere to protocol and insist on a private service rather than a public spectacle, the queen returns to London to address the nation. At Diana's funeral, Philip, William, Harry and Charles join Earl Spencer to make their infamous walk behind the coffin of the late princess.

The Truth

The events of *Aftermath* are familiar to Peter Morgan, having been covered already of his enormously successful feature film, *The Queen*. This final episode of this first tranche of four opens as phones begin ringing in the middle of the night both in the Windsor and Al-Fayed households, carrying tragic news.

In the immediate aftermath of the crash in Paris, it took emergency services more than an hour to cut the Princess of Wales out of the wreckage of the armoured Mercedes. Although it was initially reported that she had suffered concussion and broken bones, Diana had actually sustained far more serious internal injuries than anyone suspected. Upon her arrival in hospital, she was whisked into surgery; tragically, efforts to save her life proved unsuccessful. Diana, Princess of Wales, succumbed to her injuries at approximately 4.00 am on 31 August 1997.

As a devastated Mohamed Al-Fayed travels to the scene of the accident before making the unimaginable journey to the morgue to view the body of his late son, at Balmoral the royal family wait for news. Having initially been told that Diana was alive, they are informed that doctors have been unable to save her. Charles weeps and frets over his sons, who are still sleeping soundly, whilst the queen and Duke of Edinburgh make the decision to do nothing at all. They are as granite-faced as ever.

Yet whilst *Aftermath* initially paints the couple as apathetic to the point of cruelty, there was a little more nuance in their real reactions to the tragedy. The queen had been raised to present a regal, stoic face to the world and was focussed not on what the press and public thought of her, but on being a grandmother to William and Harry. Incidentally, the scenes in which Charles tell the boys of Diana's death are, as far as Prince Harry is concerned, inaccurate. Whilst *The Crown* shows Charles and William gently break the news together, Harry later recalled that Charles broke the news to him alone. Furthermore, he claims that he remained alone to brood on the loss of his mother news for hours; it is something the other members of the family have chosen not to discuss in great detail.

On screen, the moment when the queen requests that no mention be made of the accident in that morning's church service seems to suggest an emotional frigidity similar to that she had demonstrated on her visit to Aberfan. Whilst she did make this request, in reality it wasn't an act of cold-hearted disinterest, but an attempt to give the young princes time and space to process what had happened. Prince William later described the comfort he took in that service, as well as in the rugged landscapes of the Highlands. Far from disappearing and causing a domestic panic as *Aftermath* depicts, the landscape became his sanctuary.

Before this season began, much was made of the on-screen appearance of Diana and Dodi's ghosts, which sounded to audiences like a ghoulish sort of sideshow. In fact, these aren't ghosts so much as the other characters' subconscious, acting out the conversations they wish they could have had. As a narrative device they're a little bit clunky and scotch the opportunity for subtlety, sensitivity and growth. After all, how else could Her Majesty go from refusing to appear before the public to deciding to do just that in five minutes flat, if not for a masterclass in PR from the shade of Princess Diana?

Whilst the earlier episodes in this season made a villain of Al-Fayed, in *Aftermath* he is portrayed as a grieving and guilt-ridden father, shut out from the royal family despite his efforts to contact them not to capitalise on the accident, but to somehow understand and share the sorrow that he believes will unite them. The Harrod's shrine recreated here, of course, was famously very real indeed and continues to attract crowds today. In *Aftermath*, the role of villain is given instead to Prince Philip, who is a lone voice speaking out against bringing Diana's coffin home in a royal aircraft, not to mention lobbying against a ceremonial funeral and encouraging the queen to remain silent. There's no reason to believe that this is an accurate representation of the Duke of Edinburgh's response and the decision to paint him as coldly preferring to argue with Charles at a time when his grandsons need their grandfather raises eyebrows. In a series that has devoted hour upon hour to the duke's imagined angst, this is one episode where he and the queen should have been afforded much more screentime and nuance.

Meanwhile, it is Charles who lobbies for the royal family to listen to the public. He alone recognises that the overwhelming silence from the Palace will turn the public mood from grief-stricken to ugly. It is left to Princess Anne, barely glimpsed as she has been, to say what *The Crown* has been shouting for six series: the queen is no more mother to the nation than she was mother to her own children.

Whilst newspaper reports in the aftermath of Diana's death claimed that the Palace was against a ceremonial funeral, the Palace itself denied such accusations vociferously. On the contrary, both the queen and Prince Charles had always been in agreement that Diana must be given a ceremonial funeral: as the princess was no longer a member of the royal family, she did not qualify for a state funeral. In addition, whilst *Aftermath* places the decision to come to London purely on the shoulders of Diana's ghost, in the guise of the queen's conscience, Elizabeth really did take note of the growing public fury at the perceived lack of reaction from Balmoral. Her Majesty was advised by aides, officials and even Tony Blair that she must take action, but only when she was sure her grandsons could manage without her did the queen travel to Buckingham Palace.

And so, with Diana's ghost providing Queen Elizabeth II with a quick primer in what it means to be mother to a nation, Her Majesty swallows her pride, rejects her husband's warnings and goes to London. There she makes her address to the nation, whilst Harry pens the letter addressed to "Mummy" that he placed atop Diana's coffin and, as genuine news footage mingles with dramatic recreations, the boys join Charles, Philip and Earl Spencer on the long walk behind Diana's coffin. Only now, with his grandsons bewildered by the scenes around them, does Philip finally step into the role of grandfather. They're not crying for her, he tells them gently, but for you.

6.5 Willsmania

The Crown

Whilst still in mourning for his mother, 15-year-old Prince William decides to return to Eton and resume his studies. Upon his arrival, he receives many messages of condolence from his fellow pupils, but these are far outnumbered by the thousands of fan letters he receives from across the world.

During a trip to Canada with his father and brother, the reluctant William draws vast crowds of adoring young ladies, but for the shy young man, this unceasing attention is a nightmare. Struggling with the pressure, a furious William accuses Charles of driving Diana to her death, but the wise counsel of Prince Philip gives him cause to rethink his angry words. William and Charles reconcile and the young man makes a trip to his mother's secluded grave at Althorp.

The Truth

First there was Dimania then, perhaps inevitably, came Willsmania, as the late princess's eldest son stepped into the limelight in the immediate aftermath of her death. Much of this episode is broadly true, especially the feverish press and public interest in William and Harry following Diana's death. However, whilst Harry does appear in this episode, albeit looking startlingly mature for his very tender years, this is very much William's story.

When William returned to Eton College within a week of attending his mother's funeral, he was greeted by condolence letters from over half his fellow students and a sack of more than 600 letters from fans who wanted to send their sympathies to the prince. The series ably captures the sense that Eton gave William and, eventually, Harry, a sanctuary in which to grow up into young men. Just as in real life, *Willsmania* portrays William as enormously appreciative of the friendship and support of his housemaster, Andrew Gailey, who did indeed fill this position during the prince's days at Eton. Dr Gailey, an academic and respected author, enjoyed a warm reputation with his students and was a rock for William when he returned to Eton with his grief still so raw.

At a time when emotions were running high, Andrew Gailey was there to help his charge navigate the changes and challenges of life. As Dr Gailey tells William of his wife's ultimately successful battle with leukaemia, the implication is that the prince can connect more easily with the gentle and easy going academic than with his own father. We're due for another round of princely angst, but unlike the Duke of Edinburgh and the Prince of Wales, William's isn't going to occupy a whole series.

The whole crux of *Willsmania*, that people went batty for Prince William once Diana had passed away, is true. William became the focus for the affections of thousands of teenage girls, who flocked to him as though he was a pop idol or movie star. Reports regarding the young prince's attitude to the mania about him differ; *The Crown* says he loathed it, whilst other reports claim that he lapped it up or at least bore it all in good part. In truth, it's probably a little bit of all of them. The press conference he gives at Eton on his 18th birthday in this episode is fictional, though; Prince William actually gave his first official press conference a few months later, outside Highgrove.

As depicted in *Willsmania*, the crowds in Vancouver who greeted the prince during his trip to British Columbia in June 1998 are certainly an accurate reflection of the truth: wherever he went, girls screamed.

What is less likely to be true is the claim that William was furious when he learned that he was expected to do a press photocall during a family skiing trip to Canada. In reality, he would have known about the engagement long before the time came to do it. As we've already noted, photoshoots in return for a private holiday are par for the course for the royal family.

As the episode closes, Prince William visits his mother's grave on a private, secluded island at Althorp, her childhood home. Initially, Diana was to be laid to rest in the Spencer vault at the church of Great Brington, but her brother, Earl Spencer, was concerned that it would become a magnet for the princess's more extreme fans. Instead, Diana, Princess of Wales, was buried on an island in the Round Oval lake at Althorp. The grave, marked by a memorial urn, is accessible only by boat. It is a private place to which the public are not admitted.

Whilst this is a coda to *Willsmania*, it effectively brings to an end Diana's presence in this season of *The Crown*. We will briefly glimpse her again in flashback, but it is a poignant way to say goodbye to the character who, more than any other, has dominated these last two seasons.

6.6 Ruritania

The Crown

British prime minister Tony Blair is enjoying a wave of popularity that puts the royal family and his US counterpart, Bill Clinton, in the shade. Wracked by nightmares of Blair usurping her throne, the queen turns to the PM and asks for his help in winning back the love of her subjects. With the guidance of his wife, Cherie, Blair sets about laying out a series of reforms aimed at modernising the monarchy.

The Truth

In case you're wondering about the title, Ruritania was a fictional country invented by author Anthony Hope. The central European realm was the setting for his novels, most famously *The Prisoner of* Zenda, and has become a catch all for the homes of minor royals and their like.

And in this episode of *The Crown*, a minor royal is exactly what the queen feels like.

After Dimania and Willsmania, Blairmania is here and, miracle of miracles, it brings with it a political wife who is allowed to speak. First things first, let's get one thing out of the way. Surprise surprise, but Tony Blair definitely wasn't crowned king. Of course, in *Ruritania* it's all a terrible fever dream that torments the queen, who can't help but feel as the PM's star rises that a coronation might not be so far away.

Tony Blair's Labour Party swept into Downing Street on a landslide that left his opponents reeling. His approval ratings were through the roof and hopes were high for the wind of change that seemed to be blowing through the House of Commons. It wouldn't last, of course, because it never does. Not in politics.

This episode has a lot of ground to cover and it does so with aplomb, addressing as it does the UK's mission to secure American intervention in the Balkans. Blair is seeking Bill Clinton's commitment to sending American troops into Kosovo to drive Serbian forces back, but Clinton is hesitant to ally with Great Britain in case the whole thing backfires. Blair is able to swing the balance and the US/UK special relationship becomes more special than ever when, faced with the threat of American intervention, Slobodan Milosevic's forces retreat in the midst of their genocide. Hailed as a great statesman, Blair basks in international respect and stardom, little knowing that his popularity will be fleeting. In fact, Blair made such a grand and photographed entrance to the 1999 NATO summit that the other attendees sarcastically gave him the nickname, King Tony. It wasn't intended as a compliment. Yet Blair, who once scored a staggering 93% approval rating in the months after his infamous People's Princess speech, seemed to be made of Teflon.

Needing to address the worrying unpopularity of the House of Windsor, the Queen turns to Tony Blair for advice. Together with Cherie he assembles a list of reforms aimed at cutting costs, addressing anachronisms and dragging the institution of the Crown into the modern age. We are then treated to a montage of members of the royal household, each of whom holds a seemingly archaic role. In keeping with an episode that started with an elaborate dream sequence, it's all played with a nod to the absurd and a foot in the fictional. For instance, the royal herb strewer has not been glimpsed since the reign of George IV and yet here she is meeting Her Majesty, complete with a trug basket loaded with herbs over one arm and a faraway look in her eye. Yet in the end, it's the quaint anachronisms of these traditions that convinces the queen to maintain them; people don't want the mundane in a palace, she decides, they want a little bit of magic.

According to insiders, Blair really did consider the monarchy ripe for change. He believed that the royals were out of touch in the cringingly nicknamed Cool Britannia and, if some reports are to be believed, credited his team with riding to the rescue of the Windsors following the death of Diana and the public outcry at stony silence from Buckingham Palace. Of course, whilst we have certainly seen some changes in the royal family, how much Tony Blair should be credited for them is a matter for debate. He has had little to say about *The Crown* other than via an official spokesperson, who dismissed the depiction of the former PM as rubbish. That will come as a surprise to precisely nobody.

Ruritania ably nails the two faces of British power during the New Labour era, as the traditional Palace comes up against the media-savvy Tony Blair, ambitious for himself and his party and keen to make his mark on history. Yet in the queen he meets his match; she isn't at all convinced by his vision of a modernised monarchy and, it seems, neither is the Women's Institute. Cross them at your peril.

The queen was a long-time member of the WI, having first joined in 1943. She eventually succeeded her mother as president of the Sandringham West Newton branch in 2003 and, in addition to being an adored representative of the Institute, was practically its patron saint. Tony Blair, on the other hand, was a stranger to the world of the WI; perhaps that was why he made such a disastrous showing when he spoke at the Women's institute National Conference in Summer 2000. Whilst this is shown coming hot on the heels of Robert Fellowes's resignation as Her Majesty's secretary, the loyal retainer actually retired from his position in February 1999, having announced his successor, Robin Janvrin, in June 1998. However, the timeline twisting is necessary in order to contrast the queen's rapturous reception by the WI to that which greets her PM's efforts to score political points.

The on-screen Blair is slow handclapped but in fact, this is merely a small taste of what actually happened when he tested the patience of the WI. Having been warned not to make a political speech to the 10,000 attendees at the conference, Blair did exactly that. As he listed his government's achievements, the women began to heckle. When he continued, the heckling turned into slow handclapping. It was a stinging reminder for King Tony that love is rarely universal.

6.7 Alma Mater

The Crown

After Kate Middleton and her mother, Carole, have a chance encounter with Prince William and Princess Diana, Kate starts to crush on the young prince. When William begins his studies at the University of St Andrews, he finds himself attracted to fellow student Kate, but is disappointed to learn that she already has a boyfriend. At home, Kate accuses Carole of trying to set her up with William by encouraging her to drop out of her first choice of university in order to go to St Andrews, as well as pushing her to undertake the same gap year programme as the prince. Though she reconciles herself to never being his girlfriend, when Kate learns that William is considering dropping out, she asks him to stay.

The Truth

Diana's back! In an entirely fictional scene! *Alma Mater* is one of those episodes that sets out its agenda early on: we meet the characters, we're swiftly shown what they're about, then we sit back and watch the inevitable unfold. And, if it's to be believed, Carole Middleton would stop at nothing to get her daughter hooked up with Prince William.

But is it true?

Disappointingly, because it's such a bizarre moment, the scenes in which Carole and Kate happen across William and Diana selling copies of *The Big Issue* whilst doing a spot of Christmas shopping are entirely fictional. Though it lets the youngsters have a fleeting meet cute and sets Carole up as a stage mother with a vengeance, Kate never met the late princess. Instead, a 9-year-old Catherine was at a hockey match between her school's team and one that included William. The only grains of truth when it comes to the scene dramatised by *The Crown* are in Diana's passionate support of homeless charities and William's occasional forays to sell *The Big Issue* undercover. But not to Kate. As for Kate's Prince William scrapbook... sadly, probably not. As Kate herself has said, she had a picture of a Levi's model on her bedroom wall rather than a glossy of her future husband.

The background we get on the Middleton marriage is solid, with Carole meeting Kate's well-connected father whilst she was working as cabin crew, before going on to start up a lucrative business (least said about that business today), but that's not what we're here for. This is the Wills and Kate show and Wills is off to university, armed with some reasonable A-level results. As *The Crown* reports, William attained an A in Geography, a B in Art and a C in Biology, and planned to enrol at St Andrews to study History of Art, though he later switched his degree to Geography after feeling dissatisfied with his first choice of degree. However, whilst the episode depicts him receiving his exam results whilst at home with his family, he actually learned how he had done whilst in Belize with the British army at the start of his gap year. Far from reading his results surrounded by senior royals, William's A-level achievements were broadcast to the prince along with the soldiers over military radio.

We don't see too much of William's gap year, but both he and Kate joined the Raleigh International programme to undertake character building activities, enrolling just a few weeks apart. Kate had initially been due to study at the University of Edinburgh, but chose to take a year out to further her life experience. Or because her mum wanted her at uni alongside the heir to the throne. You decide. Whatever led her to make the decision, though both William and Kate undertook community work overseas with Raleigh International, they didn't follow exactly the same programme: Kate went on to study in Florence whilst her future husband found himself with the Welsh Guards in the jungles of Belize. Interesting, Wills had also been due to join the Florentine course on art history, but changed his mind late in the day. Though *The Crown* playfully suggests that this was all part of Carole Middleton's matchmaking plot, it's equally possible that it was simply a coincidence: Raleigh International has long been a popular choice even for those who aren't looking to marry a prince, after all.

William and Kate first met whilst they were living at the university's St Salvator's Hall, with Kate impressing the young prince when she modelled a now infamous see-through dress during a charity fashion show. We'll see this later in the series, but by the time we do, our fictional couple have been flirting and batting their eyelashes at one another for some time. Personally, I dearly wish that the passive aggressive librarian who inadvertently matchmakes the twosome in *The Crown* was real, but he's just a figment of Morgan's imagination, there to nudge history on its way. In telling the story of the relationship, *Alma Mater* really follows the established beats of a million romantic stories, dipping into fact whilst dolloping on the fiction, as Kate and William see their friendship thwarted by misunderstanding, feminism and other romantic interests for both. They eventually got together in 2003, but as ever *The Crown* woollies up the timeline for ease of storytelling.

Alma Mater gives William a girlfriend in the fictional shape of Lola Airdale-Cavendish-Kincaid, a name so wonderful that I wish it were real. In fact, Lola is based very loosely on Carly Massy-Birch, with whom William is reported to have enjoyed a two-week-long snog during his early student days. Loud, brash and showy, Lola is everything the bookish, sensible Kate isn't, whilst Kate's Home Counties boyfriend, Finchey, has just the right amount of smug self-satisfaction to tell seasoned romcommers with a knowing wink that he definitely isn't The One. Unlike Lola, Finchey, aka Rupert Finch, is certainly real. He and Kate dated in 2001 whilst at uni, where Finch was three years above her. Though he has never spoken publicly about the relationship, he was present at Kate's wedding to Prince William in 2011. In fact, Kate has often been seen wearing clothes from Beulah London, the fashion brand co-founded by Finchey's wife, Lady Natasha Rufus Isaacs.

There is a moment in this episode when Prince William admits to his family that he is thinking of leaving university, apparently because he's pining for Kate and can't stand seeing her with another chap. There's a grain of truth in this, as William did seriously consider dropping out after his first term, but not because he was lovesick. In fact, he found the town of St Andrews lacking in the sort of metropolitan fun that he had hoped for, whilst the ceaseless attention of starstruck fellow students was making him feel like an animal at the zoo. In *The Crown*, a combined force made up of senior royals counsels him not to throw in the towel, whereas in reality, the prince's change of heart was apparently encouraged by Charles. When William told his father that he was struggling with his course, the Prince of Wales encouraged him to switch from Art History to Geography rather than drop out. That way, William could at least see if he preferred the course before leaving altogether. The plan worked and William stayed where he was... and where Kate was too.

But there is another storyline happening alongside Prince William's romantic angst, not that we see most of it. Prince Harry, who has apparently aged at least a decade between episode four and episode five of this series, appears to be going off the rails. As William angsts, Harry is living it large, boozing and smoking weed until a furious Prince Charles insists that he go into rehab. There is some truth in that; Charles learned that Harry had been throwing wild parties at Highgrove and sent him to Featherstone Lodge for a day to get a look at the dangers of drugs and alcohol, hoping to scare him back onto the straight and narrow. Though it's merely a subplot in *Alma Mater*, it's a hint that all is not well.

But we can't let this episode pass without addressing the spectre of Carole Middleton, looming like a Home Counties Mama Rose. Was she really a puppet master, intent on marrying her daughter to a prince, or is this nothing but dramatic license? Well, as with so much, it depends who you ask. There's no denying that Carole was a hardworking woman who built her own business and fortune, no doubt imbuing a strong work ethic in her children along the way. Those same children were educated at notable schools and Kate did indeed pull out of advanced plans to attend university in Edinburgh, where she had already found flatmates and a place to live, to reapply to St Andrews in the wake of press reports that William had been accepted at the university. Whether she did it because of that is another matter altogether.

Kate and William became friends in their first year and were in a flatshare in their second, which is when they became a couple. With Kate enjoying a very close relationship with her family, it was only a matter of time before Carole was cast in the role of stage mother extraordinaire, managing every aspect of her daughter's love life. Maybe there's some truth to it, though it does rather seem to suggest that Prince William had no ability to decide his own destiny or make choices for himself. Whatever part Carole Middleton played in the early days of the romance, Machiavellian or otherwise, she could hardly have done it without two very willing participants.

6.8 Ritz

The Crown

On VE Day, Margaret and Elizabeth escape the palace and join a wild party at the Ritz, where Lillibet dances up a storm with American servicemen.

Meanwhile, in 1998, Princess Margaret suffers a stroke and her health enters terminal decline. As she and her sister recall their wild night on the town, Margaret slips away.

The Truth

Oh, how I wish the 1945 portion of this episode was true. I really, really do. But it isn't.

In a nutshell, as crowds gathered to celebrate VE Day, the two princesses sought the blessing of their parents to go out and mingle in the streets incognito. Only once they'd been granted permission did they join more than a dozen other trusted royal retainers to go first to Trafalgar Square, then on to dance at the Ritz. Among the group, as *Ritz* portrays, were Lord Porchester and Peter Townsend, but there were actually 16 people with the princesses in total, all of them considered eminently trustworthy and not in the least bit flighty. Her Majesty later admitted that she had pulled down her uniform cap in an effort to conceal her identity until one of the Grenadier Guardsmen in their party admonished her for not wearing her uniform correctly. A stickler for protocol, he refused to continue until she was dressed in accordance with regulations. Cap adjusted, the young princess sallied forth in the streets for "one of the most memorable nights of my life". Her late father, meanwhile, wrote in his diary of his joy at seeing his daughters finally able to have some fun.

The incognito royals were, for one night only, just normal young ladies. Margaret and Elizabeth, who were 14 and 19 respectively, spent the night whooping it up with revellers who had no idea that they were there. They were even among the enormous crowd of 50,000 that gathered at midnight on the Mall to enjoy a surprise appearance from the king and queen on the balcony. Little did they know it, but they might have had the princesses to thank for that: the queen admitted half a century later that she and Margaret had sent a message to their parents to say that they were waiting outside to see them. Hearing that, George VI and Queen Elizabeth came out to wave to the rapturous crowd.

Whilst the royal party didn't visit the Pink Sink nightclub in the basement at the Ritz, they did perform a conga through the hotel, causing raised eyebrows amongst some of the stuffier patrons. As images go, the heir to the throne leading a conga line past the disapproving old guard is pretty irresistible.

In counterpoint to the joyous tone of the flashbacks, *Ritz* has a rather more sombre plot running in parallel: that of Princess Margaret's declining health. As *The Crown* shows, the Queen's little sister suffered a series of increasingly debilitating strokes between 1998 and 2001, the first occurring at a dinner table in Mustique in 1998. Judging by the episode timeline, however, *The Crown* places the first attack after 2001, once Prince William has enrolled at university. The princess was already in a frail condition when she suffered severe burns to her feet as she climbed into a bath. The resultant injuries left her increasingly dependant on a wheelchair but, contrary to what this episode suggests, she had already given up her beloved ciggies years earlier.

Princess Margaret's last public appearance was in 2001, when she attended the 100th birthday celebration of her aunt, Princess Alice, Duchess of Gloucester. She died at the King Edward VII Hospital on 9 February 2002, aged 71. As shown in *Ritz*, Her Majesty's beloved friend, Porchey, had died just a few months earlier on 11 September 2001. When the queen issued a statement regarding the 11 September terrorist attacks, many speculated that her much-quoted statement, "grief is the price we pay for love" was motivated not only by the tragedy, but by her sorrow at the death of her long time friend and confidante, Porchey.

6.9 Hope Street

The Crown

Mohamed Al-Fayed makes a bombshell television appearance in which he accuses the royal family of conspiring to murder Diana and Dodi, because the princess was pregnant with Dodi's child. As a result, Operation Paget is launched; this official inquiry into the tragedy concludes that there is no merit to his accusations.

With William and Kate both single, William goes along to watch his friend take part in a fashion show. When she chooses a see through dress to model, he's smitten. However, the death of the Queen Mother sees the young prince return to London to mourn her loss just as he and Kate finally get together. Later, William chooses to visit the Middleton family rather than take part in the queen's Golden Jubilee celebrations. Yet having been reminded by them how important family is, he has a last minute change of heart and races to London to join the party. Having won her prince, Kate and William move in together to resume their studies at St Andrews.

The Truth

A note on titles: Hope Street is where William and Kate made their first home together, as second year uni students in Scotland.

In the aftermath of the tragedy that claimed the life of Dodi and Diana, Mohamed Al-Fayed devoted himself to raising awareness of what he maintained was a conspiracy to kill. Whilst the interview shown in *Hope Street* is an amalgamation of several that he undertook, the substance was always similar: Al-Fayed accused the royal family of playing a central role in the deaths. After one particularly memorable appearance on BBC Radio 4's prestigious *Today* programme, Al-Fayed dismissed the findings of the extensive French enquiry and expounded on his theory that Henri Paul was killed by MI6, for whom he had been an informer. He went on to claim that there had been a high-level conspiracy to commit murder in a broadcast that brought down a storm of criticism on the corporation.

As depicted in this episode, Operation Paget was established to examine the events of the tragic night in Paris. Heading the enquiry, Sir John Stevens eventually concluded (though not in a dramatically lit press blitz) that the findings of the investigation bore out what had already been established: namely that there had been no conspiracy and that the deaths were the result of a tragic accident. However, whilst *The Crown* depicts the investigation as taking place in 2002, it didn't actually open until January 2004, eventually concluding in December

2006. In addition, though Charles was interviewed by Sir John Stevens, the timeline in *Hope Street* has been fiddled with for dramatic effect. Charles's interview took place in 2005, when Prince William was training with the RAF. For that reason alone, the scene in which he eavesdrops on his father as he gives his statement simply couldn't have happened.

Meanwhile in Scotland, Kate is about to play her trump card. At the "Don't Walk" charity fashion show held at the St Andrews Bay Hotel on 27 March 2002, she strutted down the runway in a sheer dress worn over a bikini. The dress, designed by fellow student Charlotte Todd, sold for £78,000 in 2011 following the official announcement of William and Kate's engagement. Not a bad price tag when one considers that Todd's dress cost a measly £30 to produce and was her submission for a project entitled *The Art of Seduction*. And it's tremendously early noughties.

Eyewitnesses reported that William was bowled over by what he saw and told his friend "Kate's hot!". Lads be ladding.

However, whilst *Hope Street* sees William's happy evening destroyed when he learns of the death of his great-grandmother, that wasn't the case. Queen Elizabeth The Queen Mother died on 30 March 2002, a few days after the fashion show at which Kate made such a splash and whilst William was on a skiing trip in Switzerland with his family rather than locking lips with his new gal. The elderly Queen Mother's health had been failing for some time, but she had remained determined to continue with her duties and refused to be seen in public in the wheelchair she sometimes had to use. The doughty Queen Mother was 101 years old when she passed away at the Royal Lodge, Windsor, with Queen Elizabeth II by her side.

Prince William has spoken at length and with affection about his relationship with the Middleton family who, he insists, have always treated him as just another member of the household. He is expected to muck in with chores and relishes being part of the normal family who invited him so readily into their home. *The Crown* attempts to show that relationship to some degree, but Carole is still moving and shaking on behalf of her daughter as they gather to watch the Golden Jubilee celebrations. It's here where the episode really parts company with reality, as William is shown racing back to London to join his family at the palace. The Middletons, it seems, have taught the prince what really matters.

In reality, William and Kate still weren't a couple at the time of the Jubilee celebrations in June, and he didn't nearly miss the celebrations nor have to dash back to the capital to make a last minute appearance. Instead, William was present at each stage of the celebrations, from the luncheon to the procession to the balcony appearance in front of a million members of the public who had gathered to celebrate the reign of Queen Elizabeth II. William didn't need to race back to the bosom of his family, because he was already there.

As the episode ends, William and Kate are setting up home with their friends in Hope Street. It's a note of accuracy after a few significant wobbles. Though they'll break up and get back together, endure rumour and speculation and lots more besides, William and Kate are finally on the road to their own happy ending.

6.10 Sleep Dearie Sleep

The Crown

As Queen Elizabeth II prepares to mark her 80th birthday, she finds herself planning her own funeral. Charles and Camilla, meanwhile, would like to be planning their wedding, but the groom needs to get his mum's permission first. Meanwhile, Harry chooses to dress as a Nazi for a costume party, leading to a press furore.

Elizabeth considers abdication, but decides against it after searching her heart, and finally gives her blessing to Charles and Camilla's marriage. She selects *Sleep, Dearie Sleep*, as music for her funeral, picturing her coffin as the music plays and *The Crown* takes its final bow.

The Truth

And so we come to the end of *The Crown*. After six seasons, sixty episodes and multiple casts, Peter Morgan and Netflix's hugely popular drama of the House of Windsor is finished. Happily, it's a corker of an episode to end on in terms of spectacle and script, but how do the facts stack up?

This episode has three main strands; taken roughly in order of screentime, they are Prince Harry's ill-advised fancy dress costume, the marriage of Charles and Camilla, and Her Majesty's ruminations on abdication as she plans her funeral.

Prince Harry has never been a stranger to the headlines and his brushes with the press started early, as tales of drink and drugs were splashed across the redtops in the years following his mother's death. Yet the most furious reactions were reserved for the costume he wore to a party in Wiltshire in 2005. Warning bells should have sounded at the chosen theme of Colonials and Natives, but if that wasn't awkward enough, Harry elected to wear a World War Two Afrika Korps uniform, to which he added a swastika armband, just to be sure of dropping the biggest clanger imaginable. As shown in *Sleep Dearie Sleep*, he did briefly consider going with an RAF flight suit instead, but teenage boneheadedness prevailed. Prince William's lion costume, meanwhile, is shown as being from the same costume hire firm. In fact, he made it himself; a missed opportunity to show Wills doing a bit of crafting. Finally, if there was genuinely a drag Queen Elizabeth II present, we've heard nothing about it.

What Harry didn't expect was for someone at the party to sell a photograph of him in his ill-judged costume to *The Sun*. This august organ published it on the front page beneath the headline *Harry the Nazi*. The backlash was immediate and the prince faced a storm of criticism, with the offence caused by his costume exacerbated by the fact that it was mere weeks before Holocaust Memorial Day. Harry immediately issued a statement of apology for his actions; years later and a good deal more mature, he admitted that he regarded it as one of the most shameful things he had ever done. *The Crown* couldn't resist adding a little additional flourish, as Prince Philip telephones the costume hire company and berates them not for what the uniform represents, but for its historical inaccuracy.

Against fairly accurate scenes of Tony Blair being assailed by protestors branding him a war criminal, allegations which continue to be made against the former prime minister to this day, Charles comes to Buckingham Palace intent on securing once and for all his mother's permission to marry. As a grown man this need to ask for permission might seem bizarre, but under the Royal Marriages Act, as heir to the throne, Charles had to get the permission of the monarch if he was to finally wed his long-time love. Just like Margaret, if the queen had refused, he would have to make his request to Parliament and the Privy Council, then wait the prescribed twelve months.

In the event, as recorded in Privy Council on 2 March 2005, Her Majesty gave her consent to the engagement, which had been announced on 10 February 2005, after she had privately indicated her blessing. Over the years there has been much speculation about the queen's opinion of Camilla, whom she once reportedly called "that wicked woman" at the height of the drama between the Prince and Princess of Wales. Charles had always been unequivocal that Camilla would be part of his life and for years the couple quietly worked on winning the acceptance not just of the public, but of Charles's immediate family. It was a delicate operation that started with a joint appearance in 1999, when Charles and Camilla attended her sister's birthday party at the Ritz together, and it ultimately proved successful. Indeed, Harry spoke at the time of the wedding of how much he and his brother valued Camilla and the positive impact she had on Charles; he later was a little less effusive, discussing instead her ambition to improve her reputation at any cost. Charles himself, who has never been the most emotionally open of men, has often expressed his love for his wife, in particular the sense of humour that has carried them through trying times and into a shared future.

The Queen, however, took a little longer to warm to Camilla. She reportedly resented her for the part she played in the breakdown of Charles and Diana's marriage, but there's no doubt that that particular union was ill-suited regardless of Camilla's part in it. Of course, it was the breakdown between Charles and Diana that put the royal family on the front pages and primetime, not to mention spawned those premium rate phonelines where the public could listen to private and intimate conversations that should, in all conscience, never have been leaked at all. To Her Majesty, who had always believed in maintaining a dignified silence on matters personal, it was an alien landscape.

Yet as the years passed and Elizabeth got to know Camilla as her son's partner, relations between the women reportedly thawed, just as Camilla eventually won the acceptance of the wider public. The unofficial moment at which the queen was seen to tacitly accept Camilla as part of the family came in 2002, when she joined the Windsors at Buckingham Palace to celebrate the Golden Jubilee. Though there was still no hint of an imminent wedding, the couple's decision to set up home together in 2003 sent a clear signal of the status of their relationship to the world.

When the wedding did finally take place, in deference to his mother's feelings, Charles and Camilla agreed that Camilla would never be queen.

Instead, it was decided that when Charles succeeded to the throne, his wife would become Princess Consort. That changed in February 2022, when on the 70th anniversary of her accession to the throne, the Queen announced that Camilla would indeed become queen consort when Charles was king. It was a sure indication of her acceptance and approval of Camilla at last, ending speculation about their relationship.

In *Sleep Dearie Sleep*, Charles proposes to Camilla in a greenhouse where she, ciggie in hand, is busy potting up plants. It's a curiously charming and intimate moment in a series that has concerned itself with spectacle, but whether it's accurate or not, we just don't know. Camilla did confess that her prince had gone down on one knee, but the other details have been kept private. To seal the deal on their official betrothal, Charles gave Camilla an engagement ring from the late Queen Mother's own collection.

The couple were married in a civil ceremony on 9 April 2005, at the Windsor Guildhall. The civil ceremony was chosen in order to avoid any conflict that might be occasioned by Charles, who would later become the head of the Church of England, marrying a divorcée in a religious ceremony. It was the first civil marriage ceremony in England undertaken by a member of the royal family and was witnessed by Tom Parker Bowles and Prince William, sons of the bride and groom respectively. Neither the queen nor the Duke of Edinburgh were present. As *The Crown* contends, this was because Her Majesty wished to uphold the values of the Church of England, of which she was head, rather than because she didn't support the marriage. The official reason given by the Palace was that the couple wanted to keep their ceremony low key. However, the Queen and Prince Philip were both in attendance at the religious blessing at St George's Chapel that followed, before they hosted a reception for the couple at Windsor Castle.

Once again, *The Crown* really come up trumps in the costuming stakes, recreating Camilla's wedding and blessing looks to perfection. Whilst the full content of the queen's speech at the reception wasn't made public, there is one thing that is definitely accurate: Her Majesty really did take the Grand National as her theme. Those present have confirmed that it was a joyous occasion for all present. After thirty years, Charles and Camilla finally got their happy ever after.

The third theme of this episode is that of abdication and death. *Sleep Dearie Sleep*, the title of *The Crown*'s swansong, was also the title of the piece of music that Her Majesty selected to conclude her funeral service at Westminster Abbey. The Queen's personal piper, Pipe Major Paul Burns, played the piece after the National Anthem and before the monarch's coffin was removed for its funeral procession to Wellington Arch. By any measure, it was a fitting and respectful note on which to end *The Crown*.

In this final episode, the queen is shown planning her funeral, codename Operation London Bridge, as *Sleep Dearie Sleep* correctly notes, and musing, with the help of her younger selves, on whether she ought to stand down and clear the way for Charles to take over. Elizabeth really was deeply involved in the arrangements for her own funeral, arrangements which took more than a decade to put in place. As we see on screen, the Duke of Edinburgh was similarly involved in the arrangements for his own send-off: *Sleep Dearie Sleep* offers a glimpse of the Land Rover Defender that he selected to serve as his hearse once Operation Forth Bridge was put into action.

Despite much speculation and many acres of press on the subject, it's unlikely that Elizabeth ever seriously considered abdication. When she became queen and was anointed at Westminster Abbey, the young Queen Elizabeth II accepted that to reign was her divine duty and it was one that she intended to do for the rest of her life. As a woman of faith and a committed Christian, Her Majesty simply wouldn't have considered that the oath she made at her Coronation was one that could be broken by abdication.

To do her duty was a promise she had made to God. It was also, as history showed, a promise that Queen Elizabeth II kept from her succession on 6 February 1952 until her death at the age of 96, on 8 September 2022.

Selected Bibliography

Bedell Smith, Sally (2016). *Elizabeth the Queen: The Woman Behind the Throne*. London: Penguin Books.

Bedell Smith, Sally (2017). *Prince Charles: The Misunderstood Prince*. London: Penguin Books.

Blackwood, Lady Caroline (1995). *The Last of the Duchess*. New York: Pantheon.

Bloch, Michael (1982). *The Duke of Windsor's War*. London: Weidenfeld and Nicolson.

Bond, Jennie (2006). *Elizabeth: Eighty Glorious Years*. London: Carlton Publishing Group.

Bradford, Sarah (2006). *Diana*. London: Viking.

Bradford, Sarah (1989). *The Reluctant King: The Life and Reign of George VI*. New York: St Martin's Press.

Brandreth, Gyles (2006). *Charles and Camilla: Portrait of a Love Affair*. London: Arrow Books.

Brandreth, Gyles (2004). *Philip and Elizabeth: Portrait of a Marriage*. London: Century.

Brandreth, Gyles (2021). *Philip: The Final Portrait*. London: Century.

Campbell, John (2003). *Margaret Thatcher: The Iron Lady*. London: Jonathan Cape.

Carlton, David (1981). *Anthony Eden, a Biography*. London: Allen Lane.

Catterall, Peter (ed.) (2003). *The Macmillan Diaries: The Cabinet Years, 1950–1957*. London: Macmillan.

Crawford, Marion (1950). *The Little Princesses*. London: Cassell & Co.

Davenport-Hines, Richard (2013). *An English Affair: Sex, Class and Power in the Age of Profumo*. London: HarperCollins.

Dimbleby, Jonathan (1994). *The Prince of Wales: A Biography*. New York: William Morrow and Company.

Dutton, David (1997). *Anthony Eden: A Life and Reputation*. London: Arnold.

Eden, Anthony (1960). *Full Circle: The Memoirs of the Rt. Hon. Sir Anthony Eden*. London: Cassell.

Eden, Clarissa & Haste, Cate (ed.) (2007). *A Memoir: From Churchill to Eden*. London: Weidenfeld & Nicolson.

Forbes, Grania (1999). *My Darling Buffy: The Early Life of The Queen Mother*. London: Headline.

Hardman, Robert (2019). *Queen of the World*. London: Penguin Random House.

Heald, Tim (2007). *Princess Margaret: A Life Unravelled*. London: Weidenfeld & Nicolson.

Horne, Alistair (2008). *Macmillan: The Official Biography*. London: Macmillan.

Jenkins, Roy (2001). *Churchill*. London: Macmillan.

Junor, Penny (2005). *The Firm: The Troubled Life of the House of Windsor*. New York: St. Martin's Press.

Knatchbull, Timothy (2010). *From a Clear Blue Sky*. London: Arrow.

Macmillan, Harold (1972). *Pointing the Way 1959–1961*. London: Macmillan.

Moore, Charles (2013*). Margaret Thatcher: The Authorized Biography. Volume One: Not For Turning*. London: Penguin.

Morton, Andrew (1997). *Diana: Her True Story – In Her Own Words*. New York: Simon & Schuster.

Morton, Andrew (2018). *Wallis in Love: The Untold Life of the Duchess of Windsor, the Woman Who Changed the Monarchy*. New York: Grand Central.

Nicolson, Harold (1952). *King George the Fifth: His Life and Reign*. London: Constable & Co.

Roberts, Andrew (2018). *Churchill: Walking with Destiny*. London: Allen Lane.

Roberts, Andrew, Fraser, Antonia (ed.) (2000). *The House of Windsor*. London: Cassell & Co.

Rothwell, V (1992). *Anthony Eden: A Political Biography, 1931–1957*. Manchester: Manchester University Press.

Shawcross, William (2009). *Queen Elizabeth The Queen Mother: The Official Biography*. London: Macmillan.

Sinclair, David (1988). *Two Georges: The Making of the Modern Monarchy*. London: Hodder and Stoughton.

Thatcher, Margaret (1993). *The Downing Street Years*. London: HarperCollins.

Thorpe, D. R (2003). *Eden: The Life and Times of Anthony Eden, First Earl of Avon, 1897–1977*. London: Chatto and Windus.

Thorpe, D. R. (2010). *Supermac: The Life of Harold Macmillan*. London: Chatto & Windus.

Townsend, Peter (1978). *Time and Chance: An Autobiography*. London: Collins.

Vickers, Hugo (2000). *Alice, Princess Andrew of Greece*. London: Hamish Hamilton.

Warwick, Christopher (2002). *Princess Margaret: A Life of Contrasts*. London: Carlton Publishing Group.

Windsor, HRH The Duke of (1951). *A King's Story*. London: Cassell and Co.

Ziegler, Philip (1990). *King Edward VIII*. London: Collins.

Ziegler, Philip (1993). *Wilson: The Authorised Life of Lord Wilson of Rievaulx*. London: Weidenfeld & Nicolson.

Dear Reader,

We hope you have enjoyed this book, but why not share your views on social media? You can also follow our pages to see more about our other products: facebook.com/penandswordbooks or follow us on X @penswordbooks

You can also view our products at www.pen-and-sword.co.uk (UK and ROW) or www.penandswordbooks.com (North America).

To keep up to date with our latest releases and online catalogues, please sign up to our newsletter at: www.pen-and-sword.co.uk/newsletter

If you would like a printed catalogue with our latest books, then please email: enquiries@pen-and-sword.co.uk or telephone: 01226 734555 (UK and ROW) or email: uspen-and-sword@casematepublishers.com or telephone: (610) 853-9131 (North America).

We respect your privacy and we will only use personal information to send you information about our products.

Thank you!